MY
TECH-WISE
LIFE

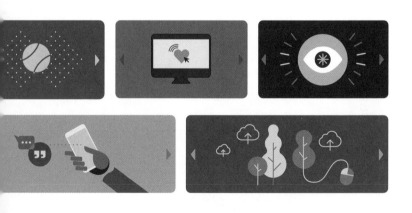

MY
TECH-WISE
LIFE

Growing Up and Making Choices
in a World of Devices

Amy Crouch AND **Andy Crouch**

BakerBooks
a division of Baker Publishing Group
Grand Rapids, Michigan

Published by Baker Books
a division of Baker Publishing Group
PO Box 6287, Grand Rapids, MI 49516-6287
www.bakerbooks.com

Printed in the United States of America

Library of Congress Cataloging-in-Publication Data
Names: Crouch, Amy, author. | Crouch, Andy, author. | Barna Group, other.
Title: My tech-wise life : growing up and making choices in a world of devices / Amy
    Crouch and Andy Crouch.
Description: Grand Rapids, MI : Baker Books, a division of Baker Publishing Group,
    [2020] | Audience: Ages 14–17. | Audience: Grades 10–12.
Identifiers: LCCN 2020018014 | ISBN 9780801018671 (cloth)
Subjects: LCSH: Internet and teenagers—Juvenile literature. | Cell phones and
    teenagers—Juvenile literature.
Classification: LCC HQ799.2.I5 C76 2020 | DDC 302.23/10835—dc23
LC record available at https://lccn.loc.gov/2020018014

The author is represented by Creative Trust Literary Group,
www.creativetrust.com.

Some names and details have been changed to protect the
privacy of the individuals involved.

Interior design by William Overbeeke

20   21   22   23   24   25   26   7   6   5   4   3   2   1

CONTENTS

a letter to Amy

Dear Amy,

As I sit here on the porch of the home where you grew up, I haven't yet opened the file you sent a few days ago with the completed manuscript of this book (complete, that is, except for my letters back to you). I want to read it—I'm eager and excited to read it—but I won't until I've finished this letter.

I want to write you this letter before I read a word, because I want you to know the most important thing I could say at the beginning of this book: you are loved.

I love you, not because of anything you've done but because you were given to me as a gift. Indeed, you were given to the world as a gift, and I believe that all that's truly good in your life is a gift.

Gifts aren't earned—I did nothing to deserve to be your father, and you did nothing to deserve to be my daughter, but we were given to one another to love. And though I haven't always loved you as well as I should, this foreword is one chance for me to do it right: to tell you you're loved, before you've done anything to impress me or earn my love.

• • •

I love you the way I loved you in the first days after you were born. You've always been a watcher, an observer, and you were such a careful observer in those first days that your mom and I actually wondered for a couple days whether you could hear sounds. You were so quiet, so still, no matter what was going on around you, even though your eyes were wide open. I remember one sleepless night, wondering if, for some reason, you would grow up without hearing, and what it would be like to be a parent to a deaf child.

The next day you startled at a noise, and we realized you could hear after all—you just liked being quiet, watching and listening. And soon enough you started babbling and then talking.

But one thing I realized during that sleepless night is that if you did turn out to lack typical hearing, we would love you just as much. In fact, I was overwhelmed by the realization that I would love you no matter what it turned out you could or couldn't do.

So I love you before I've read a word of this book.
I don't know, yet, what is in it. I'm sure there are some
parts that will make me very proud of you—but that's
not the same as making me love you more. I'm sure
there are some parts that will be hard for me to read,
moments of honesty about struggles your mom and I
never knew about, or you even hid from us at the time.
Nothing you could write could make me love you more
or less.

And I love you no matter how you sort out, exactly,
how to live in this world stuffed with technology.

I know that, like most kids and parents, you and I
may disagree to this day on where some of the boundaries should lie. But I want you to know, as we start this
book, that the most important thing is not technology
and how we use it.

The most important thing is real life—fullness of life,
"the life that really is life," as Paul wrote to his young
partner Timothy two thousand years ago.[1] It's about
growing up to do things that matter in the world, that
are deeply worthwhile—and being the kind of people
who can actually do something worth doing. And
nothing is more deeply worthwhile than love. Life is
a school of love—and family is our first school of love,
though not the only one and maybe not the last.

I'm incredibly grateful to be in the school of love
with you—one school that we'll be in for the rest of
our lives. I'm incredibly proud of the person you're

becoming. And I'm so excited that, through this book, a lot of other people will get to know you and start to imagine with you a different and better way of living the life that really is life in this beautiful and broken world.

Love,
Dad

to the reader

hello

So, you've picked up this book.

I don't know how you came across it. Maybe you spotted it on a bookshelf and wanted to hear why on earth a nineteen-year-old wrote a book about technology. Maybe a teacher recommended it to you. Or (somehow I bet this will be true for a lot of you) your parents handed it to you one afternoon.

I think I owe you a bit of an explanation for this book. Who even am I? What is "my tech-wise life" supposed to mean? What are you supposed to be getting out of this book, anyway?

Well, hi—I'm Amy! As I'm writing this, I'm nineteen years old and right in the middle of college. I'm from a small town in Pennsylvania outside the big city of Philadelphia, and you'll get to know my family—Mom, Dad, and my brother,

Timothy—as you read. You'll also find out more about what I like and how I spend my time, and I hope we can get to know each other a bit in these pages. But I didn't write this book just so you could learn about me. This book exists because of who my parents are, and what they decided to do when Timothy and I were kids.

Timothy and I were growing up right as the inventions of Silicon Valley were getting small and convenient enough to have enormous influence over our everyday lives. Computers had been around since my dad was a kid, but only recently had they become small enough to fit into a living room. Telephones had been around even longer, but they were becoming portable. TVs weren't new, either, but it wasn't until I was a kid that you could fit all of your favorite TV shows in your pocket.

Maybe it will surprise you—or maybe it won't!—that 84 percent of American teenagers have their own smartphone. Imagine: a device that didn't even exist at the turn of the twenty-first century now lives in basically every single teenager's backpack. It's an astonishing technological and sociological phenomenon. And a lot of us don't know what to make of it or how to live with it.

Throughout the book, you'll see some charts and graphs and references to data about technology usage. The data comes from a study I did in partnership with Barna Group, a social research firm that's spent a lot of time studying American teenage life. I wanted this book to not just be about *my* personal experience but *ours*. Through this data, I got a glimpse into your experiences and those of my peers who live in different places, families, or contexts than I do. Some of the data confirmed my experiences, some of it alarmed me—and some of it surprised me, as I realized that I wasn't alone in my concerns about tech.

For example, more than two thirds of teens and young adults (68 percent) agree that electronic devices keep us from having real conversations. Half of us admit we're more distracted because of technology—and more likely to put off or procrastinate on homework (yeah, that's me). More than three quarters of us (77 percent) insist that being a teenager today is more complicated than it was for our parents. And the main thing we blame that on? Technology and social media.

And I thought it was just me.

My parents had mixed feelings as they saw these developments. While nobody could deny the conveniences of tech, Mom and Dad wanted to be cautious about welcoming this brand-new force with its brand-new consequences. They didn't want to live no-tech, necessarily, but they didn't want us to regret, ten years later, the ways devices had affected us.

So Mom and Dad decided to raise us with as little tech as possible, trying to bring us up so that when we eventually started to engage with the world of devices, we would be in charge—not the other way around. And a few years ago, my dad wrote a book about it. (He does that a lot.) He didn't want it to sound like our family had no tech at all, because we had plenty; to this day, there are a fair number of devices

Setting Some Boundaries

Do/did your parents/guardians limit the amount of time you could spend specifically on social or entertainment activities (not schoolwork) on electronic devices?

By Age Group

■ Yes ■ No

13-15: 57% Yes / 43% No
16-18: 68% Yes / 32% No
19-21: 61% Yes / 39% No

All respondents, n=1,154
13-15 YO, n=289; 16-18 YO, n=351; 19-21 YO, n=514

If not, do/did you set limits for yourself?

By Age Group

■ Yes ■ No

13-15: 47% Yes / 53% No
16-18: 44% Yes / 56% No
19-21: 44% Yes / 56% No

Youth who did not have limits on social/entertainment activities on devices, n=709
13-15 YO, n=154; 16-18 YO, n=240; 19-21 YO, n=315

By Age Group

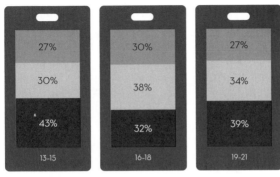

All respondents, n=1,154
13-15 YO, n=289; 16-18 YO, n=351; 19-21 YO, n=514

*What best describes what your parents or guardians do/did? (percent whose parents set time limits on **electronic devices**)*

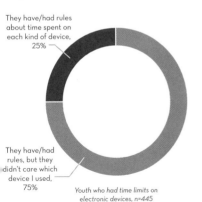

Youth who had time limits on electronic devices, n=445

*How often do you follow the rules your parents/guardians set about phone usage, TV viewing, or what you could do on your phone? (percent whose parents set rules on **media use**)*

Youth who had rules on media use, n=832

in our house. In the end, we called our lifestyle "tech-wise." Not no-tech, not anti-tech—just making wise choices about how we should live.

• • •

And now, I want to try to tell you about my childhood. About my "tech-wise" life.

But hang on—what *is* a tech-wise life?

Honestly, I often have a hard time explaining it. Growing up, tech-wise was the sum of a lot of little choices. It might be easiest to describe it by the things my family did without: no TV until I was in middle school, no smartphone until I was sixteen, no screens in sight during family dinners together, and no devices in the car. But tech-wise living was more about the things we did in place of technology. It took a while for me to figure out that there was anything unusual about the way we lived, but as you'll see, it was pretty different from my classmates and peers.

Having a tech-wise life didn't mean—and doesn't mean— I'm perfect. If you keep reading, you'll find out about a lot of ways I really messed up with technology. It's hard to be tech-wise, because it's hard to be wise.

My life looks pretty normal now. I have a smartphone. I have a laptop. I have Instagram, although I haven't posted in a year. I listen to music while I study, one earbud in and the other lying on the desk.

I live in eastern Pennsylvania, about fifty miles away from Lancaster County, where several Amish and Mennonite communities live. If we're talking tech-wise, the Amish seem to be the real deal. While it varies from town to town, most Amish don't have electricity in their homes, and almost none drive cars—you'll see them driving buggies instead. They're mostly farmers or artisans, raising corn or hewing tables by hand. And smartphones? Hard to find. Compared to this extreme, my habits with tech don't look all that unusual. Abandoning Netflix doesn't really compare to, um, abandoning *cars*. Choices like leaving my phone behind when I go to bed or losing my Snapchat streaks seem tiny.

But one of the best—and worst!—things about life is that tiny things really do make a difference. I love making bread: a bit of water, a whole lot of flour, a pinch of salt, and a teaspoon or two of yeast. I stir it all up. It forms a dense blob. I knead. Two hours later, that tough, chewy blob has bubbled up to twice its size—maybe even overflowed the bowl! When I bake it, it rises to tremendous heights, and when I pull the fresh loaf apart I see an airy crumb full of bubbles that springs back to the touch of my thumb.

If it weren't for just that teaspoon of yeast, though, my enormous loaf of bread would be a very big cracker.

So here's my hope: developing small countercultural habits might be like yeast. Small, imperfect actions can bring air and light into my life.

Baking bread takes a lot of work too. Stirring five pounds of flour into three cups of water takes muscle and a strong spoon. And kneading, while fun, is hard on the arms. But while you need this challenging, muscular work, you *also* need that little teaspoon of yeast, or else all your hard work will be for nothing.

Living wisely with our technology won't be easy. But like my teaspoon of yeast, it isn't all grand, dramatic stuff like selling your car or throwing away your TV. It starts with the tiny actions we take to shape our days. And it grows easier with time: if you knead dough only once in a great while, your arms will always get sore. If you knead every day, it'll become a breeze.

What does a tech-wise life look like? What does my tech-wise life look like? It looks a lot like baking bread: a little leavening, a lot of kneading, and patiently waiting to enjoy the fruits of my labor.

In this book, I hope we can figure out what *our* tech-wise lives should look like. I want us to think together about what tech gives us—and what it takes from us. I'll tell you about the distractions I've struggled with and the secrets I've kept. I'll tell you about my favorite thing (spoiler alert: it's sleep) and wonder with you how to tackle dull days.

But most of all, I hope you'll react. I'm not interested in giving you thirty thousand words of rules, or stories that are just going to make you yawn. I want you to think about the changes *you* have the power to make in your own life. Of course, I'd love it if you agreed with me . . . but when you disagree with me, I want you to think about why. (And tell me! But do it nicely, please.)

See, it doesn't make much of a difference if I happen to live in this weird, tech-wise way. But if you join me—if we choose to take charge of the tech in our world—it might just change all of our lives.

LESS IS MORE

There are dramatic differences in tech habits, offline activities, relationship habits, and even life satisfaction between those who use their devices less than average and those who use them more than average.

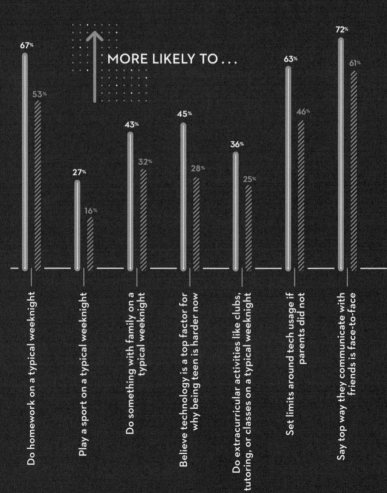

MORE LIKELY TO ...

67% · 53%
Do homework on a typical weeknight

27% · 16%
Play a sport on a typical weeknight

43% · 32%
Do something with family on a typical weeknight

45% · 28%
Believe technology is a top factor for why being teen is harder now

36% · 25%
Do extracurricular activities like clubs, tutoring, or classes on a typical weeknight

63% · 46%
Set limits around tech usage if parents did not

72% · 61%
Say top way they communicate with friends is face-to-face

6
Follow parents' tech rules most

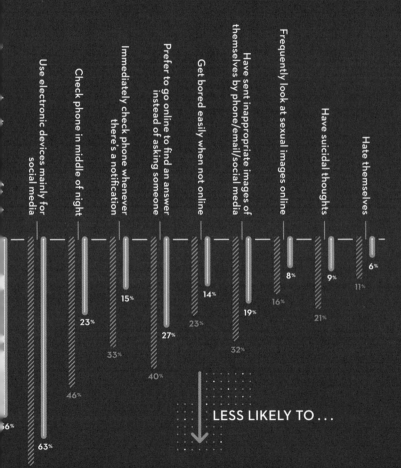

LOW-TECH USERS: Less than 4 hours on an electronic device per weekday

HIGH-TECH USERS: 8 hours or more on an electronic device per weekday

Use electronic devices mainly for social media
63%
71%

Check phone in middle of night
23%
46%

Immediately check phone whenever there's a notification
15%
33%

Prefer to go online to find an answer instead of asking someone
27%
40%

Get bored easily when not online
14%
23%

Have sent inappropriate images of themselves by phone/email/social media
19%
32%

Frequently look at sexual images online
8%
16%

Have suicidal thoughts
9%
21%

Hate themselves
6%
11%

LESS LIKELY TO . . .

n=1,154 teens and young adults ages 13–21 who own a cell phone or have access to a PC or tablet, June 26 to July 11, 2019.

we don't have
to compare ourselves

when social media freaks us out

As I scrolled through the Instagram photos, I felt my stomach churn. The first one was terrible—did my smile look that awkward in real life? Then another; my nose seemed to take up half my face. And in another one, my expression was okay, but what on earth was I doing with my arm? As I flicked through photo after photo, I started to panic.

The photos had just rolled in from a school dance, and they were full of smart suits and glittering dresses. Unlike me, my friends all looked perfect. I gazed at one friend's smile. How was it so effortless? Looking back at my own, all I saw was a forced get-me-out-of-here grin that made me look like a gremlin.

Of course, my friends all started to post on Instagram and spammed our group chat with caption ideas and gushing compliments. As they went on, I started to get more and more upset. I didn't want anyone to see these photos *ever*—if I could have stolen my friend's camera and deleted them from the memory card, I'd have been happy.

For the next few days, I kept choking up every time I opened my Instagram feed and saw other people's pictures. I was sobbing in bed and wallowing in newfound despair over flaws I didn't even know I had. And even as I was sniffling into a tissue, I was wondering, *What on earth is wrong with me? Am I really so shallow that a few thousand pixels can set me off like this?* I didn't usually obsess over my looks, and my friends always supported me when I was feeling down—why couldn't I just shrug this off?

Even now, I can't totally answer those questions; I don't think I'll ever be able to entirely unpack what was going on in my mind that weekend. But I can say something definitive about this moment: it's not unusual. In fact, pretty much everyone will experience something like this.

Now, I'm not saying you've cried over a bad photo. In fact, the thought you'd ever be upset by a picture might seem ridiculous. But it might not be about a picture of yourself. Maybe it was when you saw those videos from the party you weren't invited to, or when your friends bragged about getting perfect scores on the test you failed; maybe it's your parents' disappointment when you didn't make the team.

Whatever the cause, I know we've all been gripped by this fear that we aren't good enough. Even if we think of ourselves as confident, healthy people, we have sudden moments of terror that we'll never measure up to our friends or our family—or our enemies.

You and I aren't alone in this; our great-grandparents and their great-grandparents struggled with confidence too. Humans do this all the time—we frantically compare ourselves to others, hoping we can at least be a little smarter or stronger than someone else. But deep down, we know that there are seven billion people on earth and we will never be the best. Even Usain Bolt's record will be smashed someday.

This means that when we frown in the mirror, or wince after being embarrassed, we're in good company. But we're also especially unlucky. We happen to live in one of the worst possible times and places to be insecure—a time when we're surrounded by tech companies that make their money and grab our attention by telling us that our lives aren't enough.

Just over a quarter of Americans ages thirteen to twenty-one (27 percent) admit that when we post online, we're sometimes tempted to make things up to make ourselves seem more exciting or interesting. And for 44 percent of us, seeing other people's posts makes us feel like our lives don't match up—like our friends' lives are better than ours.

Of course, technology isn't the source of our insecurities—it's not like people suddenly started feeling bad about themselves when the iPhone showed up. But much of the technology

Social (Media) Pressure

How much do you agree or disagree with the following statements?

| Agree strongly | Agree somewhat | Neither agree nor disagree | Disagree somewhat | Disagree strongly | = 1% |

It makes feel me feel good when I have a lot of followers on social media (percent excludes those who say they don't use social media)

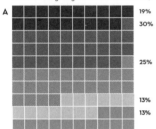

A
19%
30%
25%
13%
13%

Youth on social media, n=1,102

If I post something and don't get very many "likes" or comments, I feel sad (percent excludes those who say they don't use social media)

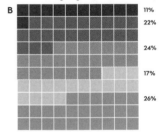

B
11%
22%
24%
17%
26%

Youth on social media, n=1,102

Sometimes when I post, I (am tempted to) make up things about my life to make it seem more exciting or interesting (percent excludes those who say they don't use social media)

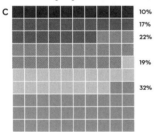

C
10%
17%
22%
19%
32%

Youth on social media, n=1,102

When I see things online about my friends or peers, I feel like their lives are better than mine (percent excludes those who say they don't use social media)

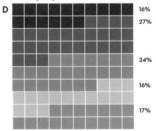

D
16%
27%
24%
16%
17%

Youth on social media, n=1,102

Sometimes it's exhausting to keep up with all the posts online (percent excludes those who say they don't use social media)

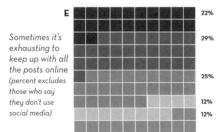

E
22%
29%
25%
12%
12%

Youth on social media, n=1,102

filling our lives both encourages anxiety and profits from it. Savvy phone companies want us to worry that our phones are uncool and out of date after two years. Free apps bombard us with ads trying to convince us that our lives are just too boring and hard.

Keeping up is hard enough—let alone putting our best face forward. Half of us admit to being exhausted by the endless stream of online posts.

Our social media feeds show us thrilling vacations and parties while we slouch, exhausted, on our couches—and then we snap pictures of ourselves when the lighting is good and pretend our lives are always exciting too.

When we engage with technology, we're surrounded by messages that our lives are missing something. Reminders of our imperfection are always lurking in our pockets.

• • •

What do we do about this? Technology isn't going to magically disappear from the face of the earth, and we don't want it to. Our phones and the internet don't just make us insecure, they also improve our lives. We can connect with far-off friends and family, we can educate ourselves on any topic imaginable, we can search for creative inspiration—not to mention the little ways tech helps, like telling us the weather, reminding us of our to-do lists, and counting our steps. Like everything in our lives, tech both helps and hurts us. So how can we appreciate the help but avoid the hurt?

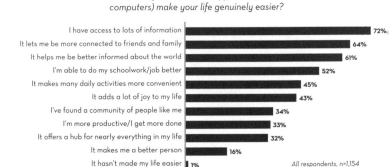

In what ways does technology (smartphones, computers) make your life genuinely easier?

I have access to lots of information	72%
It lets me be more connected to friends and family	64%
It helps me be better informed about the world	61%
I'm able to do my schoolwork/job better	52%
It makes many daily activities more convenient	45%
It adds a lot of joy to my life	43%
I've found a community of people like me	34%
I'm more productive/I get more done	33%
It offers a hub for nearly everything in my life	32%
It makes me a better person	16%
It hasn't made my life easier	1%

All respondents, n=1,154

My parents thought a lot about this when Timothy and I were little. How would they teach us to take the good and leave the bad? How could tech serve us without controlling us?

As I mentioned earlier, there wasn't a single answer. Rather, they took a number of small steps. We didn't have a TV while my brother and I were young, and when we eventually got one, we only watched movies together. We never had a video game console, either. We weren't a tech-free family, but the screens we did have belonged to our whole family, and we arranged our house so they didn't take over our living space.

Among other things, being part of a tech-wise family meant I didn't have a smartphone until high school, although I could use a computer and an iPod. I never played video games, although my brother ended up playing Wii occasionally at friends' houses. I also didn't have any social media until I was about fifteen, despite my fifth-grade friends urging me to get

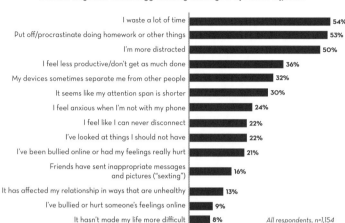

In what ways has technology actually made your life more difficult?

I waste a lot of time	54%
Put off/procrastinate doing homework or other things	53%
I'm more distracted	50%
I feel less productive/don't get as much done	36%
My devices sometimes separate me from other people	32%
It seems like my attention span is shorter	30%
I feel anxious when I'm not with my phone	24%
I feel like I can never disconnect	22%
I've looked at things I should not have	22%
I've been bullied online or had my feelings really hurt	21%
Friends have sent inappropriate messages and pictures ("sexting")	16%
It has affected my relationship in ways that are unhealthy	13%
I've bullied or hurt someone's feelings online	9%
It hasn't made my life more difficult	8%

All respondents, n=1,154

on Facebook (more about that later). While my classmates started to discover social media in elementary school, it wasn't part of my life for years.

Maybe you know what this is like; I've met a few friends whose parents had similar views on tech and social media. But this might sound strange to you—maybe really awful. Maybe you've had great experiences online and think I truly missed out. Maybe you're just confused. What did I do with my time? And maybe you're wondering if I'll start telling you to delete all your online accounts and throw your phone off the nearest cliff.

Well, I understand that confusion. Ever since my friends started to discover technology, I've had to explain my family's weird choices to people. I know these choices seem puzzling, maybe even pointless. But I hope that by sharing some pieces of my life, I might help you start to think about the role technology plays in yours. Living wisely with technology isn't one-size-fits-all; you have to do some self-searching to discover how tech will tempt you and how tech will help you.

So, while parts of my story might seem baffling at times, I hope that reading it can help you to take charge of the screens in your life. I hope you can clear away any static that technology might bring and learn to listen to your family and friends more deeply. I hope you'll discover what tech-wise means for you.

• • •

If you're pitying me for my low-tech childhood, you're not alone. When people hear about my strange family, they often worry that I missed out on television and video games and the internet. But actually, I'm struck by what I don't remember. I don't remember feeling embarrassed because I had no Instagram, or lonely because I couldn't Snap my friends. I certainly noticed that my family was unusual, but I can't find any painful memories relating to it. My friends were sometimes confused as to why I couldn't just join Facebook, but my absence from social media wasn't really a problem.

But as I grew up, I couldn't rely only on my parents' instructions. I had to figure out for myself what my tech-wise life would mean. And I can assure you that I made some mistakes along the way, which brings us back to me crying in my bedroom over Instagram.

Technology promises so much—to connect us, to save our memories, to keep us entertained. And it often delivers on these promises.

Yet it also fails.

If you've felt disheartened or disconnected by technology, you're not alone. In fact, teens who use technology a lot are more likely to say that they don't have someone to turn to for help (20 percent among high users versus 14 percent among others). Our devices aren't helping everyone connect, and they aren't making everyone happy.

In my experience, social media is one of the biggest examples of this. Its promise to help us document and share our lives is true—but it can also bring pain.

The thing is, when we try to document our lives, we start to notice that our lives are not always the best documentary material. (Some people avoid this conclusion. Their stories take five minutes to tap through and give us plentiful information about their bus ride or second cousin's third birthday. But they're rare.)

Our lives aren't always camera-ready. They're full of dreary, ordinary moments we don't especially want to remember twenty years from now, moments of exhaustion and sadness and frustration. By the standards of social media, our lives are pretty poor.

Maybe you're not too worried about how you appear on social media. I'm so glad of that. But everyone I've ever met is worried about something. We're one of the most anxious generations to date; we fear uncertain futures, worry about our present lives, and regret the past.

Again and again in our lives, we'll be overwhelmed by these anxieties and insecurities. Maybe it'll be from social media's false standards, which tell us we're not entertaining enough to be worthy. Or maybe it won't be from technology at all. But even if the source of our fear isn't technology, our devices can make it worse; in our darkest moments, our phones will nag us with constant reminders that everyone else seems to be doing way better.

So, what do we do about this? What do we do when these seemingly tiny moments tear open our scars?

Well, tech promises plenty of ways to help. The internet is a quick source of comfort. We can soothe ourselves by watching

I Often Feel . . .

anxious about important decisions	uncertain about the future	afraid to fail	pressure to be successful
40%	40%	40%	36%

*From the Barna report The Connection Generation. n=15,369 adults ages 18–35, December 4–February 15, 2019

It's clear that the comparison game is strong on social media—and brings with it both competition and insecurity. Not to mention exhaustion. More than half of respondents (51%) in the Barna survey of Americans ages 13-21 admit that sometimes it's exhausting to keep up with all the posts online. Even so, most people are grateful for all that info—nearly three quarters of respondents (72%) say technology has made their life easier because it gives them access to so much information. And while technology often gets a bad rap for separating us from other people, another frequently chosen reason (64%) tech makes life easier is by helping people feel closer to friends and family. On the flip side, no small percentage (32%) say the opposite: a difficulty they have with technology is the way it separates them from other people. In general, respondents feel more positively than negatively toward the effects of technology on their lives—but are aware that the benefits come at a cost.

someone seem even stupider and weaker than us; we can text friends; we can read over admiring comments on social media.

And this is what I tried first when I saw those photos. I texted my friends right away: "I'm just looking through all these photos, and I hate all of them. I wish I had never taken any pics." They responded quickly with love and support, telling me "You look happy and gorgeous!" and suggesting that I post to social media—"Then you'll get likes and stuff and feel validated." But even though my friends meant well, seeing their words on my phone screen wasn't enough. I was still sitting alone in my room on my phone. I wasn't comforted.

I also tried the endless stream of entertainment available on my phone; I scrolled through Instagram, watched cooking videos on YouTube, played a few games, listened to music. But entertainment only distracted me from my pain. I wasn't healed.

Here's what I hope we can commit to: when our daily troubles and lurking fears overwhelm us, let's not turn to tech.

You and I—we are broken, ragged people. We can't be healed by technology's seamless flow. We need fellowship with our broken, ragged friends.

Sharing with others sometimes feels impossible. It takes courage and vulnerability to confess our self-doubts, and it's so much easier to put on a confident face and lie. And yet the only way to find peace from our insecurities is through community.

• • •

Eventually I realized tech couldn't fix me. So I sent my youth pastor, Bethany, a text for help. I didn't say much, I just told her I was having a hard time and needed some love. We went to dinner together, and I told her about what had engulfed me, about the dark, cold place those photos had plunged me into. She embraced me, she prayed with me, and she told me about the bad photos of her own she had cringed over and the scars her self-doubts had left. We talked and wept and broke bread together.

And at some beautifully invisible moment, we both just started to laugh. We laughed because we suddenly saw the smallness of these insecurities; even the very worst pain our doubts put us through was nothing compared to the light and love of God. Three hours after I had been sobbing on my bed, broken by my ugly insecurities, I went home with a joyful heart full of the peace of community.

Please don't let self-doubt paralyze you. When you hate the skin you're in, don't gloss over it—share in person. Pray with your friends or your family. Cry together, laugh together, and remember who you truly are. This is the relief you cannot get from kind texts or viral videos or games. It's the relief you feel when you bare your wounds to someone else, and they reach out to embrace you.

Through love, not tech, we will find peace.

· ·

WHAT TO DO NEXT
Practices for Your Tech-Wise Life

» Typically, I'll use this section to give you simple, practical tips you can use right away. But the first step to being tech-wise is to think. Think about your relationship with tech. When does tech bring you joy? When does it make you anxious? What would you like to change? These questions will help you figure out where you need to take action.

» We can't be tech-wise alone. So, next, have an honest conversation with your friends or family about tech. Our use of devices has been too often shown to contribute to insecurity, anxiety, and a host of other problems. Ask questions. Listen to each other's stories. Think about the different ways you can all work on your relationship with technology.

» But as much as I hope you use screens more wisely, that's not the ultimate goal. I talked in this chapter about how screens aren't the fundamental problem; they make our other struggles and fears worse. So I want you to look beyond screens.

» I hope you can identify the people you can turn to for help, whether it's tech-related or not. Have you been struggling on your own without asking for support? I promise it'll be a relief to share what's hurting you.

» On this note, pay attention to your friends. It's easy for us to get lost in our own troubles, but we're surrounded by other people who need help. Think about how you can encourage each person you love, even when they seem to be doing fine. Offer yourself as a listener. Be the kind of friend you need.

Dear Amy,

Wow. Well, if your goal was to make me cry with the first chapter, you succeeded.

I have to admit this was so hard to read. I've never for a moment seen you as anything other than beautiful. It's painful to realize you were so distraught about how you looked to others, and maybe above all to yourself. It's wrenching to know that technology amplified all that insecurity, in spite of everything our family did to limit its effects, and that you had to bear all that alone in your room.

You are so right, though, that insecurities don't start with technology.

I think about the very first book of the Bible, Genesis, the book of beginnings. Almost every major character in it is anxious about where they fit in the world and how others see them. There's Jacob and Esau wrestling in the womb for who will be the firstborn, and Jacob scheming to cheat his brother out of his father's blessing. Before that there is Hagar, the Egyptian slave of Abram's wife Sarai, who bears Abram a son when Sarai cannot and then is cast into the wilderness with

her child because of Sarai's jealousy and rage. I suppose the story goes all the way back to the first two
brothers, and Cain's murderous fury when God favored
his brother Abel's sacrifices over his. Maybe the story
goes back further still.

And I remember my own teenage years. I was skinny
and had glasses, frequently terrible acne, and not the
greatest fashion sense. On the other hand, I was good
at school, good at music, and far, far too sure of myself
in ways that would surely have driven my friends crazy
if they hadn't been living out their own personal dra-
mas. So I swung wildly back and forth between elated
overconfidence on the good days and utter despair
that I would ever be really accepted and known on the
bad days.

This is just part of growing up. It's not the fun part.
But it is essential. Somehow I think even the stories
in Genesis are essential in that way—they show God's
people, the children of Abraham and Sarah, coming
to terms with who they really are. On the one hand
they've been singled out as the people God is going to
use to bless the whole world. That ought to give them
a sense of security and purpose. But they keep acting
in ways that undermine the whole thing, putting themselves and others to shame.

And though their foolishness wasn't broadcast in
real time the way some of our worst moments can be
today, it was somehow all remembered and recorded,

told and retold until it ended up in the Bible. Imagine having your meanest, pettiest, ugliest day, or the day of your greatest humiliation and shame, put in the pages of the bestselling book in history! It happened to Sarai and to Hagar and her baby; it happened to Jacob's sons and to their annoying younger brother Joseph. We remember them today most vividly by some of their worst moments.

As people say: awkward.

And yet, those stories are there because they are part of a larger story of rescue. One of the most amazing moments in Genesis is during the first time Hagar flees into the desert to escape Sarai's abuse. She meets an angel of the Lord, who tells her to name her son Ishmael, which means, "God hears." And in response she coins a name for God, "You are the God who sees me" (Gen. 16:13 NIV). Hagar—who isn't even part of the chosen family, who has every reason to doubt that anyone cares about her—actually comes to believe that God sees and hears her.

And when Joseph finally meets his foolish brothers who'd trafficked him into slavery near the end of Genesis, he is able to say, "You meant it for evil. But God meant it for good." Then they weep, embrace, and the brothers go home to tell their father.

I'm so glad your terrible Instagram weekend ended that way too, with a rescue: dinner with Bethany that started with tears and ended with laughter. It's really

striking that though the shame and pain could happen when you were all by yourself with just a screen,
the rescue had to happen with someone else, in a real
place, no screens involved.

As your dad, I wish I could have spared you the pain
of insecurity and the moments of pain that are still
ahead. But I'm not sure that's actually a proper or godly
wish—because it doesn't seem to be what God chooses
even for his own people, or for that matter his own
Son. If I had somehow been able to protect you from
all of that, you wouldn't ever have experienced rescue:
being saved from your worst fears, and the worst of
yourself, by someone who understood and loved you.

I think this is the real way out of insecurity: not actually being protected from it in the first place but being
rescued from it by love. Once that's happened, we can
never be quite as insecure again.

Love,
Dad

2

we don't have
to be distracted

losing attention in a swarm of devices

sat down at my laptop, getting ready to work. Now, one hour later, I'm actually starting to write.

Has this happened to you? I'm a bit embarrassed that it's happened to me (especially since I'm supposed to be writing a book about how to be tech-wise). When I opened my laptop, the notifications started to roll in. Texts I missed, reminders for a thousand different obligations, missed FaceTime calls, calendar events beeping at me. I don't know about you, but I felt like I had to answer each one. I scrolled through the texts, checked the calls, completed my reminders, and frowned at my calendar.

Then I opened my email. There's an announcement from a teacher! There's a promo code for sneakers I don't need! There's an email from every club I've ever joined, plus a few that want me to join. I archived, deleted, flicked through them all.

And here I am, an hour later, emails read and texts sent, finally clear of those distractions and about to start writing— but guess what? Another text just rolled in.

• • •

I don't know about you, but the potential for distraction is almost everywhere in my life. Unless I've turned off my notifications (which I often do, much to the chagrin of people trying to get in touch with me), my phone buzzes at me about two hundred times a day. If I need a distraction, I've got one. And I bet you do too.

Now, I'm not going to pretend that Steve Jobs invented distraction. Focusing is hard! We figure out how to distract ourselves in infinite ways—in elementary school I used to read books I held under my desk, thinking my teachers wouldn't notice I'd gotten bored. (They sent some interesting notes to my parents.)

But in our current moment, opportunities for distraction are always with us (usually in our back pockets). Many of the ways we entertain ourselves now, like books, music, and art, were once exclusive luxuries. (In the Middle Ages, for instance, just two or three books were so expensive that they were often *chained* to shelves to keep them safe![1] Yep, with literal iron chains. I hope my book ends up being that valuable someday.)

Now, although our devices are still pretty expensive, they're considered necessities. After all, most of us have them—and the average age we got them was around eleven years old. Just one app on our phones can give us access to thousands of books. If we don't want to read, we can scroll through Spotify for music; if that's not enough, we can resort to a game to engage us as much as possible—eyes distracted, fingers moving, ears full of sound.

And it's not just phones; there are countless other devices that promise to distract us: laptops, Xboxes, Kindles, TVs. See, in the dreams of Silicon Valley, we should be able to keep ourselves distracted from our distractions! (We've all seen people on their phones in a movie theater—or even done it ourselves. A thousand square feet of moving pixels isn't enough; we need to Snapchat too.)

This love of distraction doesn't just show up when we try to relax; it's also a big part of working. The flexibility and speed of our electronic devices allows us to "multitask"—to jump from task to task with a few taps of the keys. Unfortunately, this doesn't actually help us work. While multitasking, we *feel* super productive, like we're getting more work done. But in fact, no matter how productive we might feel, studies have shown that multitaskers are *less* productive than people given just one task.[2] Nearly four in ten respondents in our study (38 percent) said their biggest challenge when it comes to technology is having a harder time concentrating.

Even when we're trying *not* to multitask—to focus—our devices distract us. They'll buzz at us while we work, tempting us with something far more interesting than the tasks we're trudging through.

Are we really harming anyone by scrolling through Instagram on our bus ride? Sometimes these little distractions seem to help. They keep us busy in moments of boredom, ease awkward silences. Why should we be worried?

As someone who likes to read while I'm waiting in a dentist's office, I've been thinking about this a lot. It might help to reframe the question. What if instead of thinking about individual *actions*, we thought about our overall *posture*?

A few months ago, I noticed what happens when I sit down in a chair: I slouch. When I'm standing up, I usually have a straight back and relaxed shoulders (maybe because of all my

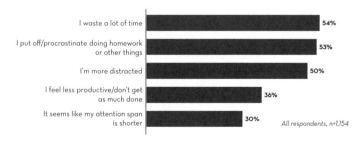

Distractions, Distractions

Because of technology . . .

I waste a lot of time	54%
I put off/procrastinate doing homework or other things	53%
I'm more distracted	50%
I feel less productive/don't get as much done	36%
It seems like my attention span is shorter	30%

All respondents, n=1,154

years singing). But as soon as I sit down, my shoulders hunch, my back curves, and my chin drops. A few hours of working like this, and my back aches when I stand up.

You'd think it would be easy to change how I sit, right? When I first noticed it, I thought it was an easy fix—I'd just sit up straighter. And then, ten minutes later, I was slouching again.

The problem is, even though improving my posture just means moving my shoulders and relaxing my neck, it's *hard* to change. I've been slouching in my chair for years at this point, I'd guess, and my body is just used to it. When I start to sit up, my body is surprised: this isn't what I usually do!

That's why I want us to think about the distractions of technology. It's hardly a problem to scroll on our phones once in a while, just as it's not going to kill me if I flop ungracefully onto the couch after a long day. But our devices don't encourage one-time, moderate distractions. Rather, they encourage a *posture* of distraction.

In default mode, our phones are constantly buzzing and beeping at us, encouraging us to spend all our time responding to them. Think about what you're doing when you kill time while waiting for the bus. I don't know about you, but I'm not sticking to one app—I'm tempted to hop from Snapchat to news to Instagram to my email. Even the time I spend on my laptop, which I mostly use for homework, is spent flicking between the zillion tabs on my browser and paging between different apps.

When we look at this on the small scale, it doesn't seem like much of an issue. Is there really anything wrong with multi-tasking? Maybe not if we do it once or twice. But I'm worried that if we don't practice focus, we'll lose it—and a life without focus is a grim one.

• • •

A year ago I witnessed a disturbing vision of what happens when we don't let ourselves focus. My high school youth group went on a spring retreat that was centered around the theme of spiritual disciplines—slow, repetitive prayer practices intended to cultivate patience and silence within. After the retreat leader introduced herself and gave a short talk, she gave us all an assignment: scatter throughout the retreat center and sit alone, in silence, for ten minutes.

Ten minutes of silence. Ten minutes of sitting in one place. Nobody else nearby. Ten minutes to sit, read a psalm, and pray.

I found my seat in a small stairwell lined with windows, and let me tell you, it was glorious. Sunlight glimmered on the tiled floors, and the gold edges of my Bible glowed in the sun. I basked in the light and felt my heart slow to a resting pace.

I walked back feeling content. But as soon as all of us gathered together, complaints started to pour in. "That was boring!" said one girl. "That was *terrifying*!" said a boy. "I couldn't sit still." "I couldn't keep my mind still." "I don't want to be alone with my thoughts, they're too painful." "I went to find my friend two minutes in."

In fact, some were crying after the stress of those ten minutes; ten minutes of no distraction, ten minutes that forced us to pay attention to what was going on in our hearts and our minds.

"I couldn't pay attention to the psalm," said one guy, "even for a minute. I just felt gross. I wanted to leave after thirty seconds."

Another, through tears: "I couldn't be alone. I just started thinking about everything I'm worried about. I couldn't get my mind off my grandma. She's sick, and I'm so scared for her."

I was horrified to realize that what could have been a time of joy had actually been a time of fear. Our ten minutes of focus had revealed that distractions were keeping my friends from noticing things that need to change. Because those distractions were helping my friends stay happy, giving them up—even to pray—was frightening. Silence had become dangerous.

And a lot of us have so much pain to carry. I was heartbroken to discover in our data how many of my peers say they *hate* themselves (19 percent), are depressed or sad a lot of the time (30 percent), or even have had suicidal thoughts (33 percent). These disheartening percentages are even higher among those who spend four or more hours per day on their phones.

Often adults complain about devices because they distract us from work: *Oh no, kids can't get their work done!* Sure, it's important for us to be able to work carefully and efficiently.

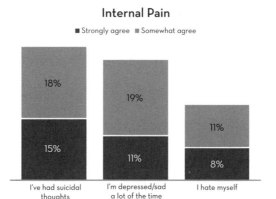

Internal Pain

■ Strongly agree   ■ Somewhat agree

18%

19%

11%

15%

11%

8%

I've had suicidal
thoughts

I'm depressed/sad
a lot of the time

I hate myself

All respondents, n=1,151 (3 respondents chose not to participate in these questions due to the sensitive nature of the subject matter)

But distraction doesn't just keep us from productivity. It also blinds us to the more serious issues of our lives, fogging over the mirror of our self-awareness. We need to be able to clear our minds and focus, or our secret fears and worries may worm their way even deeper into our hearts. Remember my story from the last chapter? I had to take my insecurity out into the light—to share it, even though it hurt.

So, how can we move forward? How can we learn to pay attention, even when it hurts?

When I was a kid, my parents did their best to keep me away from the fast-paced, always-on types of distraction that technology offers. Since we didn't have a TV for so much of my childhood, I didn't know what it was like to flip from channel to channel. Throughout most of elementary school,

I didn't go on any screens by myself, so they didn't really keep me busy. Plus, I almost never went on the internet, so I just didn't know what it was like to have billions of distracting destinations at my fingertips.

(If you ask my parents, they'll tell you this paid off. Sure, they didn't have a TV to distract us kids when they were trying to get dinner on the table, but a few years later I'd be quietly reading a book while they were cooking, not bothering them at all. And now I'm often the one making dinner.)

Plus, my parents constantly encouraged focused activities. Reading, writing, hiking, cooking, music—the kinds of wonderful things that deeply engage our bodies and focus our minds so much that they feel like play. We also often held small church services as a family, praying together and taking silence together; we'd read the Bible together and talk.

I was pretty great at focusing when I was a kid. I didn't have much of a distracted life.

• • •

My tech-wise family shaped my mind to focus. Unfortunately, the tech-crazy world made its mark too.

Looking back at my life, I see that my foundation was truly tech-wise. I always knew that the most important parts of my life—my relationships with myself, my community, the world, and God—had to exist outside of and beyond tech. I always knew that where I got real joy *wasn't* from tech. I knew from the very first that the world was enchanting and I never

needed to be bored of it. I knew everything was full of beautiful secrets, and boredom meant I wasn't looking hard enough
for them. I understood that looking closely and patiently at
the world wasn't a chore but a necessary way to uncover its
breathtaking splendor.

Tech hasn't been able to chip away at that. I know the truth
about the world. I know I don't need distraction.

But while tech hasn't taken away from my life's foundation,
it *has* built on top of that foundation. As I've had to live more
and more with technology, I've seen how easily it grows like
barnacles over my core practices and ideals, forming a sort of
blur. That's distraction.

I saw this most of all during the transition from middle
school to high school. My brother and I had shared a family
computer, affixed to a desk in our basement, for a few assignments. But around eighth grade, I started to have a laptop that
was mostly for my use, and my dad also started letting us use
his iPad when we wanted.

That period of life is in many ways about autonomy; we
slowly have to start making our own decisions, figuring out
how we'll shape our own lives. It's no longer our parents' job
to micromanage us; it's right for them to step back and let us
start to figure things out.

So I started having more freedom with devices than before. Reasonably. It's part of growing up. And I immediately
discovered their distracting lure. As I started to do homework
on the computer, my friends showed me computer games that

were way more fun. (One day of elementary school, my class entirely devoted itself to learning to play Minecraft, while our longsuffering teacher sat quietly at her desk.) And the TV shows I had watched slowly, two episodes a month with my mom and brother, I learned I could binge.

These things didn't make me happy.

See, I know, fundamentally, how I want to live. But tech has the power to distract me from it. My devices are made to do just that, so they have perfectly calibrated algorithms to keep me scrolling.

I had to slowly figure out how to deal with this. I wanted to live autonomously, but technology was getting a grip on me. So—with a lot of mistakes along the way—I started to figure out ways I could curb the distracting power of my devices. Of course, my parents helped. Dad's iPad became a tool used only in family spaces for family reasons. When I struggled to get work done, my dad told me about the strategies he used to combat distraction and work well. My mom joined me when I wanted to find entertainment in tech, and we started finding fun together.

Now, I'm still living in that tech-crazy world. But the tech-wise practices of my family have become not just rules Mom and Dad taught me but precious anchors I can cling to.

• • •

I'll pause to say that I have never tried to eliminate all distraction from my life, technological or otherwise. (There's way more to distraction than just tech.) It's not necessarily terrible to be distracted. After hours of focusing, it can be a huge relief to just zone out and ride the wave of distraction. We don't need to live a life of 24/7 focus. We simply need to avoid slouching into the easy posture of distraction. It might feel fine, but it will leave us sore.

I've found a few helpful guidelines for keeping distraction under control. The first is painfully easy: out of sight, out of mind.

It is *crazy* just how much being able to see something affects how much we use it. If I have my phone on a desk while I work, I'll think of something I should do on it. If I just keep it in my backpack, I forget my phone even exists.

Similarly, just quitting distracting apps and removing them from a device's home screen will go a long way. Before I sit down to write, I make sure to quit my web browser and messages. Somehow, the tiny, *tiny* effort it takes to launch these apps means I'm less likely to open them. And turning off Wi-Fi if I'm not working on the internet? It changes everything.

My other guiding rule is a bit embarrassing but it works: when it comes to distraction, I need to assume I have no willpower.

I don't know about you, but when I see a notification come in, I itch to look at it right away. And even if I manage not to, I'm thinking about it for the next ten minutes. If I do open it, forget about willpower. I'll look at it for "just a minute"—and then come ten minutes of texting, two minutes of looking at

Snapchat stories, and only then ten minutes of working. A homework assignment that should take one hour will take five.

Similarly, if I make it harder to access distracting things, they won't bother me. I had access to my brother's Netflix account for a few months and was shocked by how hard it was to stop watching, how easily I could just keep going without even clicking a button. I took it off my computer right away. Now, when I want to watch a show or movie, I do it with friends and family. (For example, I had a blast watching *Mamma Mia!* 1 and 2 with my friends this past spring, thanks to my friend Ellie's Netflix account.) I haven't wanted to binge-watch a show for years—because I don't have the option.

And the amazing thing is these tiny guidelines *work*. We really *can* make a difference in our ability to resist distraction.

I had a lovely, heartening reminder of this a few weeks ago. Last spring, I noticed that Instagram was sucking away my time. I'd keep refreshing my feed, wishing for something new to show up, getting bored with the endless stream of almost-identical images and videos. I didn't want to be spending my time that way! To try to break the habit, I just took the app off my phone, thinking of my "out of sight, out of mind" rule. I checked the website from time to time on my computer whenever I got curious.

A few weeks ago, I downloaded the app again to give a friend a birthday shout-out. I debated whether I should delete it right after I posted, but I figured I'd leave it up and see how it went.

Guess what? I realized Instagram wasn't a distraction anymore. I used to check it five to ten times per day, using it as a source of the distraction I craved. Now I don't feel the urge. I glance at it once a day or so and smile at the pictures of my friends. This app that once destroyed my focus is now just a pleasant, occasional diversion.

Why do these small steps help? I think it comes down to how work, um, works. It takes patience to work fast.

Now, this sounds paradoxical. But if you've played a sport—or just like to exercise—you know how this works.

I went on a forty-five-minute run this morning. For the first minute or two, it was incredibly easy! I floated down my block, admiring the roses that bloomed all around me and listening to some very cheerful birds. But as the minutes wore on, my legs started to burn and ache. My body was complaining—why was I running? Why was I doing this silly thing instead of walking? And just five or ten minutes in, my body was asking me to give up.

But again, if you've played a sport, you know how this works. Just a few minutes after the pain kicked in, my body shifted again. My feet settled into a comfortable rhythm, almost seeming to move on their own; the burning in my side seemed pleasant and ordinary. Suddenly, the hard work was normal.

This is how our minds work too. And it's influenced the way I work. When I have to do homework, I shove all my distractions out of the way—out of sight, out of mind—and I set a timer for twenty or thirty minutes. When it goes off, I'll take a break and walk around.

Has staring into our phones replaced staring out the window—have we swapped daydreaming for scrolling? The data certainly indicates that, when it comes time to "zone out," respondents are opting for screen time. More than half (53%) say they put off/procrastinate doing homework or other things because of technology. They also blame technology for feeling more distracted (50%) and less productive (36%), for wasting a lot of time (54%), and for shortening their attention span (30%). But technology is not just a distraction from work; it also offers temporary distraction from pain. And many of the respondents in the survey are struggling with real issues: suicidal thoughts (33%), depression (30%), self-hatred (19%), and more. Technology might be a good numbing agent, but given its tendency to separate people from others, it can also be a barrier to seeking the help we need.

Just like with my run, the first five or ten minutes feel impossible. How will I possibly focus for another twenty minutes? I write sentences that my fifth-grade teacher would scoff at, and I daydream.

Somehow, though, if I keep going, that feeling fades away. I get into the work. Ideas flow, the math adds up. And at the end, the ring of the timer sounds truly sweet.

The problem is, a posture of distraction makes it really hard to persevere. If we try to kill time whenever we're feeling aimless and bored, we'll never make progress. Imagine if I took a break from running every five minutes, stopping to walk as soon as my breath started to get heavy. I'd never get anywhere! And if I started to play a game of Frisbee with my friend but quit after two minutes, I'd never really start to have fun.

Developing a posture of attention means we can get over that initial hump.

• • •

Look, our lives aren't just about being efficient. I don't want you to think that the point of this chapter is just to get you to do your homework faster! Surrounding ourselves with distractions will slow us down, sure, and that's frustrating. But that's not what really matters.

Remember the story I told earlier about my youth retreat? That's the real result of distraction. We can distract ourselves from our pain and our purpose, and the result will hurt.

Honestly, when I've had a rough day, the powers of my phone and laptop are incredibly tempting. All I want to do is numb my brain and forget about everything that made my day horrible.

We might not be harmed if we do this only from time to time. But if opening YouTube is all we do to dry our tears—if we're in a posture of distraction—we'll end up burying our emotions deeply and painfully. We'll end up frightened of silence, avoiding honesty with ourselves and with God. And when we can't share our struggles, nobody can help us with them.

Let's join together in paying attention to the work we do, the pain we feel, and the beauty we see. Let's keep our devices in our backpacks, not our hands; they'll be there when we need them. Let's shift our posture.

· ·

WHAT TO DO NEXT

Practices for Your Tech-Wise Life

» Think about the times and places that tech demands your attention, and think about the steps you can take to get rid of it. During class? At work? Doing homework? Spending time with friends? Make the choice to keep tech out of sight and out of mind during these times.

» These choices look different for everyone. For instance, my friend Jeremy doesn't take his laptop home with him—he leaves it locked in the building where he works, so it can't come home with him. My friend Carley has deleted the iMessages app from her laptop altogether. And my brother, Timothy, has turned off almost all the no-tifications on his devices, leaving only the ones that signal actual messages from other people. I like to turn off Wi-Fi when I work. Be creative!

» Try going old-school. How much of your work could you do on paper, without any devices nearby? It might be more than you think. Print out online assignments, draft essay outlines on paper. Your notebook won't buzz you, that's for sure.

» Consider taking regular time away from your screens. Author Justin Whitmel Earley suggests spending an hour every day with your phone off.[3] Does this sound impossible? It's definitely unusual. But I urge you to think about spending some time without the distractions of tech. When we set our phones aside, we realize how much we haven't been paying attention to—for better and for worse.

» And setting screens aside allows us to focus on what we care about. What do you enjoy? What skills do you want to improve? By decreasing screen time, you're not leaving an empty gap in your life; you're making space for what you love to do.

Dear Amy,

Can I tell you something kind of odd about distraction? I'm actually worried we don't have enough of it.

There's a very real and disturbing phenomenon going on, as you know, called "distracted driving." Driving has become so much safer over the course of my fifty-plus years of life—both because we added new safety features to cars (a good use of technology!) and because people changed their habits (when I was a kid, for example, almost no one wore seat belts—now almost everyone does).

Driving was getting safer, that is, until about five years ago, when the trends that had all been going in the right direction started going the wrong way again.

The reasons are complicated, but it's pretty clear that distracted driving is a huge part of the problem. And no prizes for guessing what is distracting drivers the most!

Meanwhile, there is a whole category of YouTube videos that show, well, distracted everything other than driving—people so distracted by their phones that they run into and fall off of pretty much everything you can imagine.

So, why would I say that we don't have enough distraction?

Because, in one way, our glowing rectangles aren't distracting us as much as totally and completely captivating us. When we sink into the media they deliver, whether videos or games or text messages, we get totally immersed. We become very nearly not distractible.

This hardly ever happens with other things in our world. In fact, it doesn't even happen when we are using digital devices to create rather than consume. I'm writing these words to you on my laptop, sitting in our living room on a Saturday afternoon. As I write, I'm noticing all kinds of other things: the sound of the train that runs right by our house every half hour, birds sing-ing outside, and (a particularly happy sound) the clicks and clanks of you making cookies in the kitchen. I look up from the screen every few moments to glance out the window at trees rustling in the wind and our neigh-bor working in his yard.

I'm using technology, but I'm using it to create—and while I do that, I'm very aware of the environment I'm in. The act of creating focuses our attention on some-thing without taking over. In fact, we often do our best creative work in a somewhat "distracting" environment, which is why so many students go to coffee shops or libraries to work (from what I remember of college, even if libraries are quiet, the stacks full of books and the rows of desks with other students—some of them pretty cute—are plenty distracting!).

But you and I have both experienced what it's like to be consuming things on our devices. It's amazing how quickly we can lose track of time and how quickly the world around us and other people start to dwindle, dim, and almost disappear. I remember this happening to you as a child reading books (and your teachers definitely noticed it), but as we exit childhood, books stop having that total control over our attention. But screens don't. They capture us—kids and adults alike—in a way that seems almost irresistible.

And, of course, that means they distract us from other things, which is why we talk about "distracted driving." But one of the really interesting things from the research into distraction is that not all distraction is the same. Having someone else to talk to in the car, for example, is distracting (which is why a lot of US states don't allow young drivers to have more than one or two passengers). But there's quite a bit of evidence that this isn't nearly as bad for the driver as a text message showing up on their phone. (Almost every state has banned texting while driving for this very reason.) At first, this seems really weird—why would another real person, and conversation with them, not be more distracting than a bit of text coming in over a device?

I don't think anyone fully understands why, but devices are captivating in a way the real world is not. And consuming is captivating in a way that creating is not. The most captivating thing you can do is consume on a device—so captivating that if you get caught in its clutches, you'll lose track even of the absolutely essential thing you mean to be doing instead, like not walking into a lamppost.

And I guess the exact opposite would be creating in the real world. So what would be the opposite of captivating? I guess it would be liberating.

This is why I love your decision to keep distracting, consumption-oriented devices out of reach and out of sight much of the time. By saying no to them, you're saying yes to the real world and real people, with all their healthy distractions—and freeing yourself to actually create something new with the people around you.

Love,
Dad

we don't have to be disconnected

scrolling alone

I've tried to forget most of the details of middle school—who needs to remember the most awkward years of their life? But I do vividly remember one day from seventh grade, a drive home on an average Friday. I had recently inherited our family's ancient iPod with the little circle wheel (have you ever seen one of those? One of my friends called it a "museum piece") and had taken a pair of family headphones with me. I had to wait alone for my dad to pick me up—he was getting my brother from somewhere else—so it was the perfect opportunity to listen to some music.

Eventually he pulled up to the curb, right as a song was ending, so I pulled off the headphones and got in the back seat (Timothy had claimed the front seat). He asked me about my day, and I told him it was fine. He said his day had been fine too. We didn't have much to say.

I thought I'd put my headphones back on and keep listening to my music; nothing interesting was happening. But the moment I put them on, my dad noticed and looked over his shoulder. With a stern face but a twinkle in his eye, he told me to play my song for the whole car to hear. "That's not supposed to be an iPod! That's a *we*Pod!"

Yep, he's pretty great at dad jokes.

But even if it's silly, I think Dad's joke helps illustrate a crucial problem of technology: our devices can distract us not just from ourselves but also from the ones we love.

Now, I want to be careful here; there are a lot of angry adults going on tirades against us teens, declaring we're doomed to be mindless zombies staring at our phones all the time. This is unhelpful and ridiculous. When we use our devices, it's not because we hate our friends or think they're boring—it's because we sense an awkward silence, because we want to check why our phones buzzed, or just because there's something cool to look at. Sometimes we turn to our distractions, and sometimes we're totally engaged with the world around us. And just as with adults, there's usually a reason we want to distract ourselves.

I didn't pull out my iPod because I wanted to be rude to my dad and brother; in fact, I wasn't really thinking about them at all. I just wanted to listen to some music, so I turned it on.

That said, I'm grateful for my dad's silly joke. It reminded me that while it's not wrong to use our devices by ourselves, there's a more excellent way. When we share what we're enjoying with others, we open up far more possibilities.

● ● ●

If you made it through the last chapter, you made it through a long discussion of distraction. I mostly focused on distractions in trying to get something done; when we're trying to work, sleep, or drive a car, technology can be a menace. But our devices aren't only hindering productivity. They get in the way of much more important things—not just homework but fun and rest and love.

For instance, think about when you're hanging out with friends. Haven't you noticed how quickly people pull out their phones, hoping to find something more interesting? It usually happens with good intentions—someone wants to show everyone a funny video or their latest post. But once the phone comes out, it stays out. And once one person is on their phone, it feels so much easier for the rest of us to follow suit.

I notice it when I'm doing things for fun too. By this point you're probably not surprised that I like to read. Yet if I have my phone nearby, even if the book is riveting, my mind wants distraction. Despite the fact I'm *enjoying* what I'm doing, my brain wants something new! I see the notifications and long to open them, even though I know they're probably not very important.

I'm not alone in this: nearly four in ten of the respondents in our survey (37 percent) admit they get bored easily when they are not online.

Sociologist Sherry Turkle has identified what she calls a seven-minute rule in conversations: "If you want to be in real conversations, you have to be willing to put in those seven minutes" before taking out your phone or moving aside.[1] Basically, our conversations with others will inevitably start out with boring chatter about the dull details of weather, homework, and what's for lunch. It takes time, attention, and patience to dive into what we really want to talk about. To be a good friend, I can't distract myself during those chats about the rain—ignoring the boring stuff is ignoring the opportunity for real connection.

We all *know* this to be true, but we're all guilty of doing it—68 percent of us readily admit that electronic devices keep us from having real conversations. And half of us see phones as a significant disruption to our family meals.

The thing is, none of us *want* to ignore our friends. None of us go into a conversation thinking that really, scrolling online would be more fun. But we need to recognize that when conversations lose out to phones, everybody's missing out.

And it's so much more fun to be engaged—laughing my head off at an inside joke from a friend is way better than snorting at a clever Tweet. So, how can we be more engaged and less distracted?

• • •

I got an unexpected clue to this question from a lunch date with my grandparents.

We went to the same diner we always go to—a small wooden building with flower baskets under the windows called Hank's Place. Hank's looks pretty normal from the outside, but once you walk in and see the newspaper and food magazine cuttings hanging on the walls, you know it's special.

And then you see the menu! The menu at Hank's, as at any good diner, is ridiculously long and features everything from hamburgers to Belgian waffles to mushroom strudel. That day my granddad got a grilled Reuben sandwich, my grandma got a BLT, and I tried the mushroom ravioli. (Small distinction of my home: we live very close to the Mushroom Capital of the World, a town called Kennett Square, where the mushroom geeks live and produce over half of America's mushroom crop. Yep, thrilling. Come visit me anytime.)

All the servers know my grandparents' names, and our orders are often a bit delayed by their questions about old high school friends and about when my grandparents will come to Hank's next. I always have trouble choosing a dessert, so I end up asking them for recommendations.

I think you can see why we love this place.

A few weeks ago, though, I started to appreciate it in a new light after I went to a Panera.

I was waiting for a friend and put my bag on a table to claim it. I hadn't been there for a while, since it was a bit out of my way. I could have ordered at the counter, but I didn't; I headed over to a self-serve kiosk. I scrolled through the endless variety of soups, decided that maybe I wanted a salad instead, then realized I wanted a sandwich.

Once I had paid, I grabbed a buzzer, and somewhere behind a tall counter, an employee I couldn't see got my order and put it in the line. I went to sit down and then headed to the other end of the restaurant when my buzzer beeped, just in time to see a disembodied hand push my sandwich onto a high counter.

On my way back, I happened to glance over at the cashiers, caught a glimpse into the kitchen—and saw a familiar face!

As it turned out, my friend Cleo, who I hadn't seen in months, was working there over the summer; she'd been the one to put my sandwich on the counter. We both gasped and waved frantically—it had been too long. I ran up to the counter and we had a rapid conversation before more customers came. We were both thrilled.

Now, I don't want to bash Panera, or other fast-food places like it, too much. I have to thank them for introducing me to the bread bowl, which is a genius idea if you ask me, and it's a good place to grab a quick bite. But the fact is, I could have spent my entire visit to Panera without knowing my friend

Cleo was there, even though she was serving me my food! In fact, fast-food restaurants are designed so I don't notice people like Cleo at all—so that I can order food and pick it up without being slowed down by a single person anywhere.

And this is facilitated by technology. Of course, the walls built around the kitchen and the height of the counter aren't technological. But thanks to the kiosk, I can order without talking to or seeing anyone. Thanks to the buzzer, there are no servers to ask how the food is or recommend desserts.

Contrast with Hank's. At Hank's, the whole place is constructed to remind you that there are people there and that they're important. The kitchen is right in front of you when you walk in, and there aren't walls around the first section—you see people making waffles and scrambling eggs. You're greeted right away as you pick a table, and if your server knows you, he or she knows the table you usually like. Servers are constantly coming around, taking people's orders and carrying their food, chatting with you and checking to make sure your meal is good. And when you're done with your meal, you head up to the counter—by the waffle-makers—and pay a cashier right there.

These two places both want us to enjoy good food in a pleasant place. Panera has nice fireplaces, cozy chairs, and lovely paintings on the walls; they certainly aren't trying to ignore customers' needs. But at Hank's, the people making your food are there and ready to love you. At Panera, technology hides the workers from view, even your old friends.

Phone Time or Meal Time?

Do family members bring phones or other devices to meals with them?

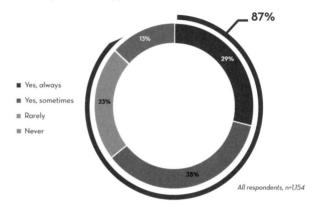

87%

- Yes, always — 29%
- Yes, sometimes — 35%
- Rarely — 23%
- Never — 13%

All respondents, n=1,154

How often do you or your parents/guardians use their phones at the table during a family meal?

(percent among those whose family members bring devices to meals)

Comparison

■ You ■ Parent/Guardian

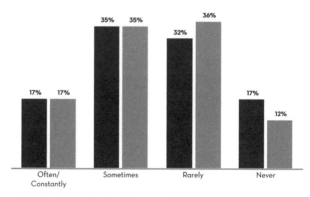

	You	Parent/Guardian
Often/Constantly	17%	17%
Sometimes	35%	35%
Rarely	32%	36%
Never	17%	12%

Youth whose family members bring devices to meals, n=1,005

If you put all the Hank's people—the cooks and owners and servers—into the Panera space, they'd be stuck behind walls too. And if my friend Cleo started working at Hank's, she wouldn't be hidden behind high counters. She'd be out and about, chatting all the time with people.

This is how much spaces can shape us. The priorities of both a sit-down restaurant like Hank's and a fast-food place like Panera affect us through the design of their physical spaces.

Guess what? We have the opportunity to do the same thing! We get to build our lives around whatever we choose—that's what growing up is about. We get to decide what is most important in our life.

The problem is that our technology doesn't always prioritize this. Most app developers, for instance, are primarily thinking about how they can keep you using their app; connection with others is a secondary value.

Sometimes, shaping spaces is literal. For instance, consider my family's house.

If we've cleaned recently, you won't see any devices at all when you walk in. You'll see a lot of childhood artwork by Timothy and me, some bookshelves, a bunch of couches where we sit and talk and read, and a woodstove that keeps us cozy in the winter and uses up wood from fallen trees around us. If you go upstairs (again, this is in our freshly cleaned utopian house), you still won't see any devices, nor any charging cords for them. Our kitchen off the hall has one counter where all our phones go, plus an iPad where we keep recipes. If you're feeling silicon-deficient, you can go downstairs, where we stash all our family tech (including the elusive TV).

Of course, if you walk in on a typical day where we haven't cleaned up, it won't be such a pristine, tech-free space. My laptop will probably be on a couch-side table, and my mom's will be too. Upstairs there might be a phone or two.

The point is, at the end of the day when I'm getting ready for bed, or in the afternoon when I want to chill on the couch, my laptop and phone have their own specific place—and it's *not the same place* as where I rest or where we spend time as a family. When I want to read, I'll often put my phone in its little kitchen nook; you can bet it goes there when I head to sleep too.

Chances are you could do this too. Where do you hang out with friends? Is it your bedroom? The kitchen? The family

I Wish Our Family Spent More Time Together and Less Time on Our Devices

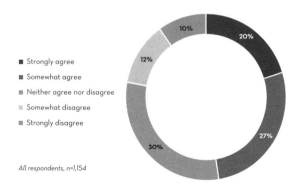

- Strongly agree
- Somewhat agree
- Neither agree nor disagree
- Somewhat disagree
- Strongly disagree

All respondents, n=1,154

10%   20%   12%   27%   30%

room? How could you shape that space so that technology doesn't hide people, your friends?

Your house probably isn't exactly the same as mine. Maybe it's way bigger or way smaller, or you have a tiny living room or a huge yard. Here's where we can all get creative. My family puts most of our tech in one room in the basement, but what if you approached it differently, perhaps by making one specific room a low-tech zone? Or put up notes in every room with favorite tech-wise activities? Think outside the box.

But a lot of our time spent with people isn't at home. It's at school, at work, on the athletic field, at a coffee shop. In these cases, we don't have a huge amount of power to shape the spaces (although if you do have that kind of power, go for it—and tell me all about it!); we're pretty passive within them.

What can we do? Well, we can choose where in the space we're going. For instance, my favorite pizza shop is a fabulous place—except they always have a TV on above the bar, showing the sports game. Now, this is local spirit! We get to watch our local teams play! But when I sit with people near a TV, I notice our eyes are *constantly* drawn to it. Our little magpie brains see something shiny and fast-moving and *bam*, there goes our attention. So what can we do? Find a corner where there isn't a TV in our line of sight. Or, if we're brave enough, we can turn the TV off. (Environmentalist Matthew Sleeth does this whenever he's in a public space with a TV, and advises us all to follow suit.[2] He says, "Not once has anyone objected," but I've never quite worked up the courage.)

We can also decide how we behave in that space. When hanging out with friends, it's worth making a commitment to keep phones away.

• • •

I was struck by the results in the data to a series of questions that contrasted what we'd rather do with what we *actually* do. The majority of people readily asserted they'd rather talk to friends in person than text them, go outside rather than stay inside and be online, spend time with family rather than spend time online, and so on. However, in all these cases, people also had to admit that they *actually* tended to do the opposite of what they desired to do. Most of the time, they chose the digital option.

Phones like to sneak in.

One Friday night last year, I was baking some scones with a few friends. We had stirred up a simple maple-banana batter (it sounds ridiculous, but I promise it's delicious), pressed the sticky dough into a disk, and cut it into neat triangles. When the scones came out of the oven, they were glistening so gorgeously that we all pulled out our phones to document the occasion—it would be a travesty to forget about such beautiful baked goods! I liked the scone picture I'd taken and decided to put it on my Instagram story, just so everybody else could know I was having a much better Friday night than they were. I had to swipe through a bunch of filters before I posted it, of course, but decided it looked better without, and

Would You Rather?

What would you rather do?

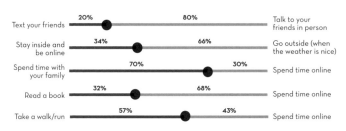

All respondents, n=1,154

What do you actually tend to do most often?

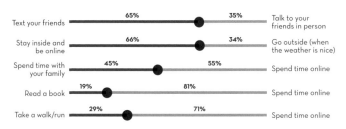

All respondents, n=1,154

then when I posted it I figured I might as well look at everyone else's pictures, and then—hey, look, there's a notification from GroupMe! I decided I'd better check my group chats.

(By the way, three out of five people [60 percent] do this: they immediately check their phone whenever they hear a notification.)

At some point I finally looked up. My friends were talking to each other and enjoying their scones. I had isolated myself—totally unintentionally. I was staring at my phone while my friends were right next to me.

We need to be able to gently call ourselves out when this happens. Not beat ourselves up, for sure; I know that when I pull out my phone, it's not with malicious intent. When I check my phone or pull out my laptop, I have a whole list of justifications ready. I'm making lunch plans! I'm checking my astronomy homework! Chorus rehearsal might move!

We also need to extend this grace to others. Honestly, that can be pretty hard. A few years ago, I came late to school lunch after a wrenching confrontation with a teacher. I sat down next to a friend, longing to get everything off my chest.

But she was texting her mom. The friend next to her was also looking down at his phone, scrolling through Instagram. I said hello and they said a distracted hello back. They didn't notice the just-dried tears on my cheeks.

And you know what? I had to offer grace that day. I had to acknowledge that I, too, had missed out on things because of my own distractions. I had to forgive them, just as I would have wanted them to forgive me.

I wish I'd thought of preventing this kind of thing ahead of time. For instance, I've heard of people making a pile of phones in the middle of the table at school lunches, so nobody touches theirs. Could you challenge your friends to do this with you?

It is clear from the data in this chapter that technology—phones, in particular—are causing relational tension and frustration. Phones have become a ubiquitous part of every social gathering, even family gatherings. The majority of families bring phones to the dinner table (64%). And for respondents who live on their own, it's even more likely they bring their phone to the table when they eat with friends (67%). However, there is clearly an awareness that this is not the ideal: nearly half of respondents (47%) say they wish their family spent more time together and less time on their devices. Even more telling is the clear desire to choose people (and nature and exercise) over technology, countered with people's reality—in which they admit that, in actuality, they more often choose technology.

We should also be wary of photos taking over. (Unless you're doing a photoshoot!) I like to take photos, for sure. It's great to commemorate our most precious moments, and it's a delight to look back on them. However, I've noticed that there's an inverse rule involved: the longer you spend fussing about photos, the less fun everyone has. If there's a moment you want to capture, go for it—but make it quick and choose not to worry about the outcome.

It's also a good principle to put your phone on silent when you're with someone. Now, I know we always worry about emergencies; my phone has a setting where I can choose whose calls/texts will come through even when it's silent. A few times in my life, I have been interrupted by a very important call while I was hanging out, and I was very glad I picked up the phone. But it's rare, and there are not many people who would contact me for a true emergency.

• • •

Look, if we shape our lives to look like a fast-food restaurant— like a Panera—it's not the end of the world. We'll still have some relationships, and we'll still enjoy some of the fruits of life.

But our lives *could* be like Hank's. Our lives *could* be shaped so that relationships, not devices, are at the center. We can choose to welcome our friends into our hearts; we can set aside the screens that can separate us.

WHAT TO DO NEXT
Practices for Your Tech-Wise Life

» Where do you spend your free time? Your bedroom? The den in your house? Your favorite coffee shop? Do what you can to shape these spaces.

» Have a conversation with your family about tech's proper place in your home. What technologies help you connect with others, and which make you draw inward?

» As always, don't be restricted to my suggestions; be creative! But here are some ideas to riff on: don't have chargers in your bedroom so that tech won't linger there; fill your room with non-tech activities you enjoy. If you have a TV, move it away from the center of your house—make room for other kinds of fun. Set up a central charging station where everyone's devices can go "to bed" at night.

» Talk with your friends about what technology means within your friendships. Is it helping you connect? Is it distracting you from each other? Talk about how you can lovingly call each other out when someone prioritizes tech over friendship. Perhaps you could make a pact with all your friends that you'll put tech aside while hanging out, or pile your phones in the middle of the table when you're eating lunch.

» Consider your own behavior. Are you really engaging personally with friends? Timothy points out that interactions such as posts and anonymous comments are pretty impersonal. What if you focused on personal communications like texts, calls, or video chats?

» Try repurposing the tech you use alone. Prone to bingeing on TV? Have movie nights with your friends instead. Love scrolling through Instagram? Use the posts you see as reminders of those friendships; reach out in person/online instead of just liking and moving on. When we use tech alone, we're ignoring its real potential. Let's think outside the box.

Dear Amy,

I'm at the end of the chapter, but I'm still thinking about the beginning—where you accused me of telling a "dad joke." Ouch! I've always tried to be above that level of humor. I guess dads are not a good judge of our own jokes.

But while it may have been a clunky attempt to be funny, I actually want to stand up for my idea. That iPod, ancient scroll wheel and all, ought to have been called a "wePod" all along.

Everything around us is designed. Designed by someone, for a particular reason, in ways that shape how we act and react. And we have decisions to make. We can just blindly accept the designs that others have made for us, or we can actively try to redesign the world—whether it's the name of a device or how we do lunches at school.

Someone designed the iPod, including its name— actually a team of someones. One of the key designers who worked on that original iPod was a man named Tony Fadell. He went on to be part of the original iPhone team, and then started a company called Nest

that designs devices for the home (in fact, a Nest ther-
mostat is one of the very few devices visible on the
first floor of our house!).

Why did Tony Fadell and his team design the iPod to
be used by a single person, with headphones, instead
of by a whole group of people? And why did they call it
an iPod, anyway?

Here's the really fascinating thing: music used to
be a lot more like Hank's than like Panera. Hank's is
shared, community-oriented, a bit noisy, and a bit cha-
otic, with no walls separating people from each other.
For almost all of human history, that's what music was
like. Music was made out loud. It was something people
created (rather than consumed) and something they
did together (rather than alone). In fact, when I was a
child, even when people listened to music, they did it
together—look at photos or videos from the 1970s and
you'll see handheld "boom boxes," the cassette tape
players with big speakers people carried around.

All that changed when I was a teenager with the
introduction of the Sony Walkman. It played the same
cassette tapes that the boom boxes did, but it was tiny,
just a bit larger than a cassette itself, and it came with
headphones. Suddenly music, which for all of human
history had been shared, became something private.

And people loved it. Because there's something
about us that likes being in charge of our own world—
being able to choose our own way and not having to

share it with others. This is part of an even larger story, the story of "individualism" in the Western world: our tendency to want to design our lives ourselves. Once individualists had experienced the privacy and autonomy of the Walkman, they didn't want to go back.

One question in your survey revealed this very clearly: when asked what a typical weeknight at home looked like, the majority of respondents (69 percent) said it looked like everyone just hanging out—doing things on their own.

The designers at Apple Computer (as it was called back then) understood this better than almost anyone, and that's part of the reason they started naming all their products with the letter i (which also stood for "internet"). First came the iMac. Then the iPod. Then the iPhone and the iPad. I, I, I . . . do you see what they were doing? They were designing. They were choosing to reinforce something and make it easier—our desire to be "I," me, all alone, not responsible to anyone else (and not bothering anyone else either).

But every time you design to make one thing easier, you make something else harder.

Here's one more interesting thing about Tony Fadell. A few years after he worked on the iPod and the iPhone, he gave an interview to the magazine *Fast Company*. And in that interview, he talked about being a dad with kids and watching how dependent they were on their smartphones—the very devices he'd

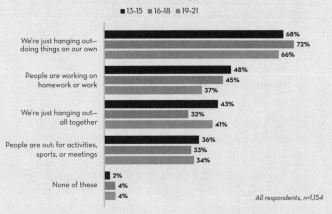

In Your Family, Does a Typical Weeknight at Home Look Like Any of These?

■ 13-15　■ 16-18　■ 19-21

We're just hanging out—
doing things on our own
- 68%
- 72%
- 66%

People are working on
homework or work
- 48%
- 45%
- 37%

We're just hanging out—
all together
- 43%
- 32%
- 41%

People are out: for activities,
sports, or meetings
- 36%
- 33%
- 34%

None of these
- 2%
- 4%
- 4%

All respondents, n=1,154

designed. He wasn't entirely happy with what he had made. "I wake up in cold sweats thinking, what did we bring to the world?" he said.[3]

When even the guy who designed the thing wakes up in the middle of the night worrying about it, maybe someone ought to redesign it.

I love a lot of things about our devices. But I wish Tony Fadell and his team had designed them for we and us rather than for I and me—designed them to help connect people rather than separate them. (With their iOS 13 operating system, Apple did take a step in this direction, making it much easier to share audio with a friend, at least if you both have a pricy set of Apple's AirPods. And even without extra hardware, apps like FaceTime can be great ways to connect across long distances.) That's why I insisted, even to the point of painful dad jokes, that in our family we'd take these things and redesign them. Even if the iPod was designed to be used alone with headphones, we'd redesign it and use it as a wePod.

There's a word in the tech world for this act of taking something and finding opportunities to use it in ways it wasn't originally designed for: hacking. Hacking can be destructive, but it can also be incredibly creative.

And so, I love the suggestions you have in this chapter for how all of us can do some redesigning. We don't actually have to totally accept the world as it was designed for us—we can redesign it to make sure it actually is good for us and our relationships.

In making the choices you describe here—like peering over the wall at Panera to talk with your friend, even though the whole restaurant was designed to frustrate that conversation—you're thinking like a designer. Or a redesigner. Or, maybe, a hacker. I suspect Tony Fadell would be proud.

Love,
Dad

we don't have
to live with secrets

hiding with tech

D o you remember when phones had passcodes?

You might be too young. But I vaguely remember that to unlock the first iPhones, you had to put in a four-digit passcode. Click the home button, swipe the little bar to the right, and tap four digits.

Then came the six-digit passcode—way harder to guess. Unfortunately, whether you had four digits or six, the phone auto-locked after too many failed guesses, which led to a real nuisance if a mischievous younger sibling got hold of it.

And then came the fingerprint. No more typing in a passcode! Once you'd entered your fingerprints into the phone's log, you'd just tap your thumb to the home button and the phone would unlock.

And now it's faces—your face gets scanned. My own phone is five years old, so I'm still stuck on unlocking with my thumb, but I'm impressed whenever I see someone just *look* at their phone to unlock it.

Why such advanced locking systems? These changes show us just how much our relationships with cell phones have shifted. If someone stole my flip phone in 2014, they wouldn't have had to hack through any password protection, but they also wouldn't have found out much about me. They'd see texts asking my mom to pick me up or telling a friend I was on my way to lunch. They would have known what school I went to and possibly figured out my home address, but there wouldn't be that much to steal. (Professionals, on the other hand, had password-protected Black-Berries throughout the 2000s. But those were for lawyers and politicians.)

If someone could hack into my smartphone now? Yikes. They'd get hold of my banking information, they'd be able to read all my emails, and they'd see every photo I'd taken for the past few years. They might be able to log into my personal accounts on various websites, thanks to the passwords I have saved. They'd also be able to read the personal texts I'd sent to my friends and family; they'd be able to see who I'd been talking to and who I'd ignored; they'd be able to see all my social media activity.

My relationship with my smartphone is nothing like my relationship with a flip phone. My phone is no longer a tool with limited skills; it's a log of my life that needs serious protection. It's tied to my own fingerprint, and it holds pieces of me.

As a result, our phones now contain far more security technology than before. We have the tools to hide whatever we like. Our phones are small; they hide in our pockets, opening only to our fingerprints or faces or passcodes. We can hide our activity from people who are in the same room. We can open private tabs on the internet and clear our history, making it seem like all our activity is gone with a click. And we can easily block people from viewing our social media profiles and from sending us texts and emails.

• • •

These tools are incredibly important; if we're going to store so much of our lives on these tiny little glowing rectangles, they'd better be well protected.

But while I'm a fan of privacy, there's a fundamental contradiction here. Sure, there's a veneer of privacy over our devices and internet use—but it doesn't go that deep.

Why? You've probably been reminded about it a million times. I know I have. My school librarian was in charge of teaching internet privacy to freshmen, and I overheard her lessons many, many times while catching up on work in the library. Dry erase marker in hand, she'd warn the class: don't do *anything* online you wouldn't want your grandmothers to see, or advertised on a billboard, or whatever the cliché of the day was.

I remember one exercise where students had to analyze social media profiles as if they were college admissions officers. Bobby bragged on Twitter about getting a speeding ticket in his new car, but Jamie posted on Instagram that he'd spent the day handing pizza to homeless people. If you were a college admissions officer, which one would *you* let into Harvard? You get the idea.

Now, by this point in my life, I'm pretty sick of hearing adults lecture me about the internet. Simplistic lessons like the ones I overheard in the library don't reflect the real world. However, they are based on a grain of real truth.

Our activity and our data are surprisingly accessible to strangers. First of all, huge corporations can access our emails, social media posts, and internet history, although these might be anonymized, and sell them or use them to target us with specialized ads. They're also often accessible to hackers—companies like Capital One and Target have had customer information stolen. And even conversations that seem like they should be private, like texts or DMs, are easily screenshotted and sent to people who *definitely* weren't supposed to see them. (At least Snapchat and Instagram tell you if someone's taken a screenshot. But somehow that's scarier.)

This is the weird paradox of technology: while it's easy to hide parts of our lives from people close to us, it's harder to keep them safe from strangers. If we want to keep secrets from our family or friends, our devices will help. We can change the passcode on our phones or go in private mode on our computers with just a few taps. But those secrets, while perhaps anonymized, are accessible to anyone with enough knowhow. And, as I heard over and over from my librarian, our layers of anonymity can be easily peeled away.

This is the *opposite* of what we want.

See, privacy is super important. I'm not a big rule breaker (as my more adventurous friends will confirm), but I definitely don't want to be spied on even if I'm just reading a book or climbing a tree. We can't be independent if we're always being watched. (There are deep philosophical arguments for privacy, and I could have a *long* conversation with you about this, but I think we can agree that having strangers spy on us is just creepy.)

But with the people we're close to, like our family and friends, I've become convinced that unlimited privacy is not best for us. Don't get me wrong; we need some privacy in our close relationships. However, when privacy gets extreme, we get *secrets*—parts of our lives that we desperately seek to hide.

Our devices make pretty great secret-keepers. But our lives shouldn't be secretive.

• • •

One of the biggest secrets our generation keeps? Porn.

Whatever your relationship to pornography might be, you definitely know someone who looks at sexual images on a computer, tablet, phone, or other device regularly; 30 percent of our teen respondents say they look at porn either frequently (9 percent) or occasionally (21 percent), and an additional 24 percent say they do so rarely. And a lot of people come across pornography by complete accident (62 percent)—there's just so much sex on the internet that it shows up even when you aren't looking for it.

Even more common than watching porn is sexting. Researchers typically group this in with pornography, calling it "self-pornification." About a quarter of the teens and young adults we surveyed (24 percent) have sent inappropriate images of themselves to someone by phone, email, social media or app, and of those, 56 percent did not feel "at all guilty" about doing this. And while the majority of people have never sent sexual images of themselves, 27 percent of them still say someone has asked them to do so.

Online sex, whether personal sexting or porn on the internet, is an unavoidable influence on what being a teenager means today. And its overwhelming effect on us is one of the few things we can clearly trace to technology. There is nothing in human history like the unlimited access to pornography that sits in the back pocket of almost every American child.

This kind of enormous change calls for serious thinking. How should we relate to sex in the modern world?

I think we need real caution, because the privacy paradox is especially dangerous when it comes to sexuality. Our phones

Forbidden Images

How many people in your circle of friends do you think regularly look at sexual images online?

Legend: ■ All of them ■ Most of them ■ About half of them ■ A few of them ■ None of them ■ Refuse to say

	All of them	Most of them	About half of them	A few of them	None of them	Refuse to say
Female 19–21	12%	25%	12%	29%	16%	6%
Male 19–21	20%	27%	13%	19%	13%	7%
Female 16–18	6%	23%	15%	31%	18%	6%
Male 16–18	14%	22%	13%	25%	17%	10%
Female 13–15	1%	9%	17%	29%	36%	8%
Male 13–15	7%	16%	14%	33%	22%	7%

Have you ever accidentally come across any kind of sexual images on a computer, tablet, phone, or other device?

Legend: ■ Yes ■ No ■ Refuse to say

	Yes	No	Refuse to say
Female 19–21	65%	31%	4%
Male 19–21	69%	28%	3%
Female 16–18	62%	33%	5%
Male 16–18	57%	33%	10%
Female 13–15	62%	30%	8%
Male 13–15	59%	30%	10%

How often, if ever, do you look at any kind of sexual images on a computer, tablet, phone, or other device?

Legend: ■ Frequently ■ Occasionally ■ Rarely ■ Never ■ Refuse to say

	Frequently	Occasionally	Rarely	Never	Refuse to say
Female 19–21	5%	22%	29%	37%	7%
Male 19–21	16%	30%	26%	21%	7%
Female 16–18	7%	20%	23%	42%	8%
Male 16–18	13%	24%	23%	26%	13%
Female 13–15	1%	11%	20%	60%	8%
Male 13–15	10%	18%	21%	37%	14%

All respondents, n=1,151 (3 respondents chose not to participate in these questions due to the sensitive nature of the subject matter); Male 13–15 YO, n=191; Female 13–15 YO, n=95; Male 16–18 YO, n=175; Female 16–18 YO, n=176; Male 19–21 YO, n=239; Female 19–21, n=275

Sexting

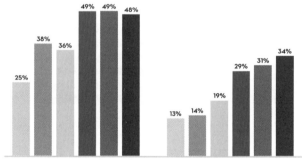

Legend:
- Male 13-15
- Male 16-18
- Male 19-21
- Female 13-15
- Female 16-18
- Female 19-21

My friends have sent me inappropriate images of themselves, by phone, email, social media, or app
- 25%
- 38%
- 36%
- 49%
- 49%
- 48%

I have sent inappropriate images of myself to someone by phone, email, social media, or app
- 13%
- 14%
- 19%
- 29%
- 31%
- 34%

All respondents, n=1,151 (3 respondents chose not to participate in these questions due to the sensitive nature of the subject matter); Male, n=605; Female, n=546

■ Male   ■ Female

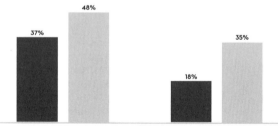

* I felt guilty about sending inappropriate pictures of myself to someone. (very + somewhat guilty)
- 37%
- 48%

** I have been asked to send an inappropriate picture of myself, but I chose not to (percent among those who have not sent this type of image)
- 18%
- 35%

Youth who have sent inappropriate images of themselves, n=451; Male, n=291; Female, n=160
**Youth who have not sent inappropriate images of themselves, n=766; Male, n=433; Female, n=333

and computers make it easy to watch porn and send nudes secretively—but our devices are also frighteningly insecure.

At my middle school—and pretty much every other one, from what I could tell—kids' pictures got screenshotted and sent to one person, and then a bunch more, and then everyone. You'd frequently hear a few giggles in class as someone opened an explicit Snap under their desk. If you were unlucky, you'd get a random pic from someone you almost never talked to.

Is this a healthy way to live? I don't think so. If we share the most intimate details of our lives with tech, our private lives may suddenly turn public—perhaps even without our knowledge. But our generation is regularly doing just that. I'm afraid it will come back to hurt us, and already has.

Now, it's no surprise that, as teens, we're drawn to explore sexuality. Our teen years are a time of crazy hormones and plenty of curiosity about sex. Sexuality naturally shapes our lives as we grow up—although it doesn't by any means define us, and our own attitudes about sex will vary pretty widely from person to person. Our desire to explore this fundamental part of life makes sense.

But we need to recognize how much sex can hurt us. I don't feel comfortable sharing my friends' stories here, but I don't need to. I fear that you all know stories of the ways sex can scar us. I pray that none of you have a story like that yourself, or ever will have.

Sex is a part of life, yes, and it's a part of life we need to take seriously. And to do this, I don't think we should just rely on ourselves or the internet. Rather, we need to be grounded in healthy relationships with trustworthy people. We need friends who will hear our stories and keep them safe. We need significant others who will listen to our boundaries. I urge you to think about how comfortable you feel sharing honest questions and experiences around sex with your friends. Are your friends a safe place to go, or would you think twice before confiding in them?

As great as our friends are (or should be), though, the perspective of adults can be necessary. I feel pretty lucky that, whenever I needed it, my parents were willing to have conversations about sex. Awkward? You bet. But I had real questions and needed real answers. Although we didn't exactly talk about sex at the dinner table, I'm grateful my family was willing to have honest conversations with me. I hope your family will

Sex Talk

How often would you say your parents/guardians talk(ed) about sex with you?

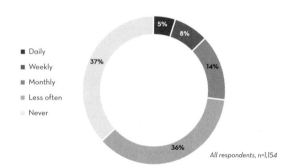

- Daily
- Weekly
- Monthly
- Less often
- Never

5%
8%
14%
36%
37%

All respondents, n=1,154

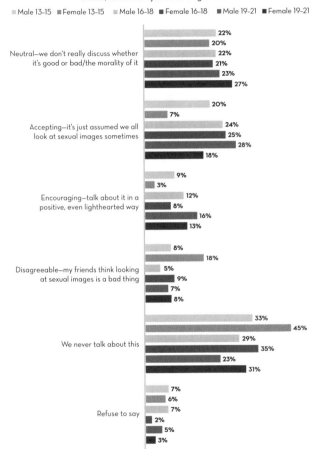

When your friends talk about looking at sexual images online, is it most often in a way that's . . .

■ Male 13–15 ■ Female 13–15 ■ Male 16–18 ■ Female 16–18 ■ Male 19–21 ■ Female 19–21

Neutral—we don't really discuss whether it's good or bad/the morality of it
22%
20%
22%
21%
23%
27%

Accepting—it's just assumed we all look at sexual images sometimes
20%
7%
24%
25%
28%
18%

Encouraging—talk about it in a positive, even lighthearted way
9%
3%
12%
8%
16%
13%

Disagreeable—my friends think looking at sexual images is a bad thing
8%
18%
5%
9%
7%
8%

We never talk about this
33%
45%
29%
35%
23%
31%

Refuse to say
7%
6%
7%
2%
5%
3%

All respondents, n=1,151 (3 respondents chose not to participate in these questions due to the sensitive nature of the subject matter); Male 13–15 YO, n=191; Female 13–15 YO, n=95; Male 16–18 YO, n=175; Female 16–18 YO, n=176; Male 19–21 YO, n=239; Female 19–21, n=275

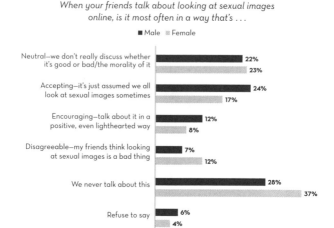

When your friends talk about looking at sexual images
online, is it most often in a way that's . . .

■ Male ■ Female

Neutral—we don't really discuss whether
it's good or bad/the morality of it
Male 22%
Female 23%

Accepting—it's just assumed we all
look at sexual images sometimes
Male 24%
Female 17%

Encouraging—talk about it in a
positive, even lighthearted way
Male 12%
Female 8%

Disagreeable—my friends think looking
at sexual images is a bad thing
Male 7%
Female 12%

We never talk about this
Male 28%
Female 37%

Refuse to say
Male 6%
Female 4%

All respondents, n=1,151 (3 respondents chose not to participate in these questions
due to the sensitive nature of the subject matter); Male, n=605; Female, n=546

be there when you need them—no matter how awkward it
might feel.

But not everyone has people like this. Your family might
have shut you down when you tried to talk to them about
sex. Your friends might not have been willing to listen to you.

The internet seems like a secret, easy way for us to deal with
our sexual desires and questions ourselves. We don't even have
to deal with other people or tell anyone else about it. It makes
sense—after all, we google everything else.

I wish it worked as well as googling "how to tie a tie." But
I'm afraid that far from being an innocent resource, the internet is a seriously flawed place to seek knowledge about sex.

The internet is saturated with sex. Unfortunately, online porn doesn't represent healthy sexual relationships any more than a show like *The Office* represents a normal, healthy workplace. Pornography on the internet is engineered to look like fun, casual sexual encounters, but it's as fake as it gets—and portrays demeaning and cruel behavior. Explicit content doesn't portray loving relationships; it shows underpaid actors putting on a show for large corporations.

And online porn can show truly unacceptable sexual behavior. One study found that 33 percent of popular online porn clips contained physical or psychological aggression. You aren't getting a balanced view, either. In over 90 percent of these clips, the woman was on the receiving end of the violence; one researcher described the world of internet porn as "a male-dominated porn industry shot through a male lens."

What happens if you experience sex through staged, male-dominated, violent content? Unfortunately, though it's fake, this kind of content affects real people in the real world. A survey of teens found that "of the roughly half who had seen pornography, 53 percent of boys and 39 percent of girls said it was 'realistic.' And in the recent Indiana University national survey, only one in six boys and one in four girls believed that women in online porn were not actually experiencing pleasure."[1] Porn isn't real, and in most porn, pleasure and pain are entirely staged.

But if we believe the lies of pornography, real people will get hurt. I saw this at my school. I found out that guys who seemed harmless had treated girls aggressively. Classmates discussed uncomfortable sexual experiences in hushed tones, and, later, in louder ones—asking an adult about it would have been unthinkable. Girls posted long captions on their finstas confessing that last night had been a nightmare.

Ironically, our secrecy is undermining our privacy—and our ability to love those around us.

• • •

What does healthy privacy look like for us?

We have to strike a thoughtful balance. I'm grateful I can say that there's nothing on my phone or my internet usage I'd feel ashamed of showing my family. But despite this, I don't want my parents scrutinizing my every move. Part of growing up is gaining autonomy—being able to do things like browse the internet or go into the city by myself. If my parents were checking my web history every day, they'd be treating me like a child. In other words, privacy comes with growing up. We become responsible for our behavior—we, not our parents, are in charge of monitoring ourselves.

But too much privacy isn't what we need either. What happens when privacy gets compounded over and over, layered into perfect secrecy? It's not good.

Extreme privacy looks like anonymity—your behavior is completely split from your person, and nobody knows who you are. If you do something wrong, they can't trace it back to you.

Anonymity offers freedom, and freedom feels *good.*

Sometimes this looks harmless. A moody teenager posts anonymous poems with no worries about what his classmates might think. A student complains about her teacher on Tumblr. A fan of *Game of Thrones* whines about the plotline of the final season.

But anonymity also frees people to create terrible, terrible things. Have you noticed the recent trend of YouTubers reading their hate comments on video? Anonymous commenters don't care about the humanity of the person they're attacking; they craft their insults like bombs. Mobs can form online; in an infamous incident in 2014, thousands and thousands of male video gamers crafted a horrific harassment campaign against women in the industry. Their targets had to move multiple times and conceal their identities due to death threats.[2] And the internet can foster depraved extremes of radicalism, such as the shooter in Christchurch, New Zealand, who posted his white-supremacist manifestos before committing his crime.

This is what happens when there are no consequences, and it's bad. The way to healthy privacy is not through anonymity.

Instead, I think it's based on trust.

As I write, I'm sitting in my bedroom with the door closed. Nobody else is in the house. My parents are both at work, taking it for granted that I'm doing nothing they'd be ashamed of, such as reading radical terrorist manifestos or bullying five-year-olds. This is because they trust me. They've spent a lot of time teaching me what is right and wrong, and I've done my best to live up to it. My privacy comes from the trust they have in me.

At the same time, though, my relationship with them is honest and open. They know the passwords to all my devices and accounts (at least, I've told them many times). If they wanted to, they could log on to my computer and search my browser history.

Yet if they actually did this every day, our trust would be broken too—in a different way. If my parents trust me, they shouldn't *need* to be checking my location every two minutes to make sure I haven't run away to join the circus. Lacking trust can seriously strain a relationship, and it's crucial for us to cultivate relationships with enough trust that privacy is possible.

The sad result of not enough privacy is secrecy. Some people I know change their passcodes constantly, clear their browser history, and even hide their devices so their parents won't snoop. Because they aren't allowed any privacy, they resort to deception to gain some privacy back.

I think we can have both privacy and openness. And I think that looks like accountability.

In my family, we tried to structure our use of screens to avoid secrecy. Not without security, of course—when my brother and I got phones, email accounts, and laptops, we immediately set up passcodes and fingerprints. But we also shared our passcodes with our parents right away. Mom and Dad friended us on social media and can see our posts (although unlike some parents, they haven't gotten around to Snapchat).

Online Privacy

At home, I use my computer in a space where anyone can see it

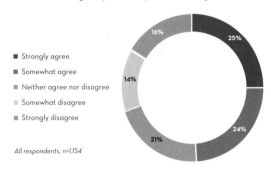

■ Strongly agree
■ Somewhat agree
■ Neither agree nor disagree
■ Somewhat disagree
■ Strongly disagree

All respondents, n=1,154

I don't keep my passwords a secret from my parents/guardians

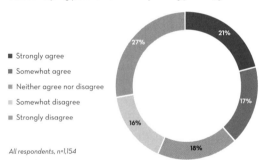

■ Strongly agree
■ Somewhat agree
■ Neither agree nor disagree
■ Somewhat disagree
■ Strongly disagree

All respondents, n=1,154

And before we had our own devices—for most of my life—my brother and I were using shared family devices that both of our parents had full access to (and control over). We did homework on the computer anchored to our basement; it couldn't come into our own bedrooms.

But perhaps this wasn't quite enough. While I haven't hidden pornography or radicalism or cyberbullying, I did keep some secrets.

In middle school, my brother and I shared access to my dad's iPad, where we could access TV shows and movies. I've mentioned before that on the occasions we watched TV, it was together and slowly. When I began to have this access to a portable device that I could hide in my room, I realized I could binge-watch episodes without my family. I desperately procrastinated, watching episode after episode, losing sleep until I was exhausted.

But a few weeks in, my mom noticed the iPad was missing from its spot. She had also noticed I'd been distracted and absent. She then noticed I'd caught up on *Doctor Who* without her. So she confronted me, gently, one day in the kitchen, as I was about to sneak away to try to watch another episode.

I don't remember the details of the conversation. I do remember the deep sorrow in her voice, the worst not-angry-but-disappointed emotion possible. Why, she wanted to know, hadn't I shared? Why hadn't I opened up to her and told her I was losing so much time to this? My dad was disappointed that I had tried to hide it, that I had snuck around my parents' backs.

Dad didn't want my secrets to injure our family. If I kept going behind their backs, I'd end up resenting Mom and Dad. I'd hide more and more important things from them. This was a pretty minimal secret, but if I'd kept it, I would have gone

Ruling on Technology

Do your parents/guardians have any rules about . . .

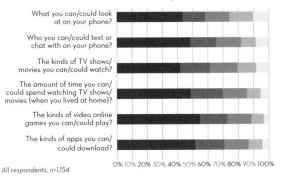

■ No rules ■ Very flexible rules ■ Somewhat flexible rules
■ Somewhat strict rules ■ Very strict rules

What you can/could look
at on your phone?

Who you can/could text or
chat with on your phone?

The kinds of TV shows/
movies you can/could watch?

The amount of time you can/
could spend watching TV shows/
movies (when you lived at home)?

The kinds of video online
games you can/could play?

The kinds of apps you can/
could download?

0% 10% 20% 30% 40% 50% 60% 70% 80% 90% 100%

All respondents, n=1,154

How do you feel about these rules?

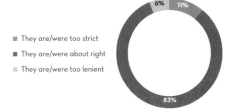

■ They are/were too strict
■ They are/were about right
■ They are/were too lenient

6%   11%

83%

Youth whose parents set rules on media use, n=832

on to keep bigger and bigger secrets. And what would be left? Fear and suspicion.

Most of the things we hide are, like my TV bingeing, small and boring. And I think we should be wary of those small secrets. Sure, I don't do anything on my laptop that I wouldn't want to see on a billboard. But that doesn't mean I don't use tech to hide stuff. While I don't have any particularly shocking secrets, I am constantly tempted to use tech to hide my everyday weaknesses.

For instance, tech is by far the easiest way to hide procrastination. And I must admit, I'm deeply tempted to procrastinate. I'm a pretty optimistic person by nature. I like to think I can get a twelve-page paper done in an hour. (Spoiler alert: I can't.) Why not do something fun instead of starting the work early?

Tech gives me opportunities to hide all the time I'm wasting. When I procrastinate by reading a book on the sofa, my parents can tell I'm not working. But if I'm sitting at the table with my laptop, my family can't see whether I'm working hard or ignoring my responsibilities. Even studying across from a friend won't help!

This isn't the kind of secret that would make a college admissions officer reject me—it's the kind of secret that quietly ruins my working hours. It doesn't seem like a big deal. But if I do it for nineteen years, it will become one.

Worse, though, are the deep vulnerabilities I try to hide with tech. There is no easier way to hide pain and sorrow than

It's no secret that the internet has amplified pornography—the amount of it, the access to it, the ability to hide it, and even the inability to hide ourselves from it (62% of respondents say they have *accidentally* come across porn online). It is perhaps not surprising to see that porn use becomes more common as young people get older—nor that boys are viewing sexual images online more often than girls. The prevalence of porn has also led to more acceptance of it. Just 9% of respondents say that when they talk with their friends about looking at sexual images online, it's in a disagreeable way. For most, those conversations are neutral (23%), accepting (20%), or even encouraging (10%). However, a good chunk of people admit they never talk about it with their friends (33%). They also don't talk about it with their parents: 37% say their parents never talk to them about sex, and an additional 36% say their parents talk with them about sex less than once a month.

through devices. When I'm hurt, the quickest fix is scrolling through my notifications and giggling at the memes in a group chat or flicking through my emails. I can usually get my mind off whatever's bothering me.

And then, when I come home from an exhausting day of school or a wrenching confrontation with a friend, I can use technology to help me lie. After a moment of calming myself down on the web, I can fake it. "Oh, you know, I have a paper due tomorrow, but I'm doing okay!" Never mind that I'd cried in the library, that I'd spent hours on work but had hours more to go, that I'd struggled with all my practice tests and all I wanted to do was go take a nap.

These are not shocking things. They're not scandalous. That's because we're not always hiding scandals with our technology. Often we're just concealing the mundane foibles that are an unavoidable frustration of humanity. But we need to pay attention to the things we hide, even if we tell ourselves they're not that serious.

• • •

I need people to see through my secrets.

I need study buddies to check on how I'm working; if I don't have them, I might just while the hours away and lose time and sleep. I need my brother to give me advice when I'm stuck so I don't give up in tears. I need to tell the secrets of my procrastination and to share the foolish ways I've wasted time.

And I need the people who love me to see through my cheery mask; I need them to tell me that no, I'm not okay, and I need to talk. I need my friends to call me out when I try to shove my troubles under the rug. I need the strength to confront the fears that gnaw.

Why? Because of my Christian faith, I believe that people who see through me are actually acting in the image of God. The biblical figure Hagar gives a name to God that illuminates this: He is "the God who sees me."[3]

I believe we're called to do as God does. We're called to see and be seen by each other, as much as it may hurt us. Those we love are best equipped to understand our temptations and steadfastly hold us accountable. They can point us to the One who sees us.

It can be uncomfortable and inconvenient to be known; sometimes it's terrifying. But it's better than keeping secrets in the dark.

. . . .

WHAT TO DO NEXT
Practices for Your Tech-Wise Life

» Make a plan with your family about practicing privacy. Try figuring out appropriate boundaries with your parents— which passwords they will see, how often they should check up on you, what you should trust each other to do. Be honest with your family if you feel they're being overly controlling (or overly lax).

» Consider sharing your passcodes with someone whom you trust to keep you accountable. Phone passcode, computer password, logins to social media.

» Talk about what you see on the internet with people you trust. Share both what you enjoy and what makes you uncomfortable, and listen to them in turn. Teach and learn together. (Try including your parents on this!)

» Consider moving devices to public spaces when possible. Working? Watching TV? Browsing the internet? Being around people you trust and respect will help you stay accountable—and is way more fun.

» Timothy reminds me that there's no such thing as real digital privacy—on the internet, there's always someone watching what you do. How does this change your behavior? What do you have to do differently when your phone is public, not private?

» More wisdom from Timothy: if you find yourself thinking your parents might not approve of something you're doing, ask yourself why. What concerns might your family and friends have? Should these concerns prompt a change in your behavior? If so, how can you put them into practice and perhaps ask for help?

» Most of all, pay attention to your secrets. They might be scandalous and they might be mundane. Choose to do the hard work of sharing them. I promise it's far better to bear burdens with someone else.

Dear Amy,

Speaking of secrets: I think by now you and I, and our readers, have a secret in common—something almost no one who hasn't read this book will understand.

This book isn't really about technology.

Of course, technology is part of it. But what is clearer and clearer as I read each chapter is that this book is really about something much bigger than our devices.

And I think in this chapter you're onto something especially big: the idea that privacy is good but secrets are not.

This is so fundamental. I wish I had learned this much earlier in my life. There is a lot that I keep private—many things only your mom knows, or only a few close friends know. But I am relentlessly trying to eliminate secrets from my life—things that only I know (and, I suppose, that God knows, whether I tell him or not). Nothing good in my life has ever come from having secrets.

Your description of the ultimate secrecy—what happens when we become totally anonymous—is spot-on and scary. Anonymous literally means "without a name." No one was ever meant to be "without a name."

It's actually interesting how many of God's interactions with people involve calling them by name—from God calling out, "Adam, where are you?" in the Garden (as Adam and Eve are hiding—one of the first attempts at secrecy) to Jesus saying, "Mary," in the garden with the empty tomb. We are meant to be named.

This is one way technology really has changed our world. Technology has made it strangely easy to become someone "without a name." And that explains so much of the sadness and loneliness—also the hostility and danger—of life online. When you are without a name, you may feel very free but are actually cut off from yourself, other people, and God. Of course I understand that in hostile environments, there can be safety in anonymity, but most online anonymity isn't really like that. Or maybe we want to be anonymous online because we sense there really isn't anything safe about a space where it's so hard to be truly known.

I think in a way anonymity is the end result of the "individualist" life I wrote about at the end of your last chapter. There may be good reasons for us not to want a boom box life, blasting everything about ourselves to everyone around us. But we also should flee a life of total isolation, the life lived entirely between a set of earbuds and in front of a screen only we can see. You could call it iLife. Actually, a friend of mine named Dale Kuehne wrote a whole book about it called *Sex and the iWorld* (because one of the things that gets most distorted in the iWorld is sexuality, the part of our lives that is meant to involve being most deeply known). It's not real life at all (and it's not real sex, either).

And that's why this book is not really about technology. Because the only way to be really known, known by name and known well, is to leave the privacy of our devices behind and tell our secrets in person to friends and family we can trust. It is absolutely amazing what happens when we do that.

Not everyone feels like they know anyone they can trust with their deepest secrets. Sometimes naming the hardest truths of our lives without our names attached can be a first step toward healing. But real healing ultimately leads to real relationships. If the only place you share the deep secrets of your life is online, anonymously, they'll just grow in destructive power. But share them in person, face-to-face with someone whom you know loves you, and the things that seemed so powerful when they were secrets burn away like mist, leaving behind real love.

Technology sure makes it easier to go down the path of anonymous secrecy. But it can't bring us back home, back to life. Only real love can do that. Fortunately there are still people and places in this world where you can find that kind of love. I will keep praying for you, that you'll find those places and create them for others.

Love,
Dad

86% I check my phone first thing in the morning.

WITHIN THE FIRST HOUR OF THE MORNING, I . . .

86% Check my phone

Eat breakfast

31% Check my email

23% Exercise

Pray

17% Do homework

15% Read the news

Read a book

7% Meditate

6% Read the Bible

Journal

ILL NIGHT

80% I check my phone right before bed.

32% I check my phone in the middle of the night.

IN MY BEDROOM AT NIGHT, I FREQUENTLY . . .

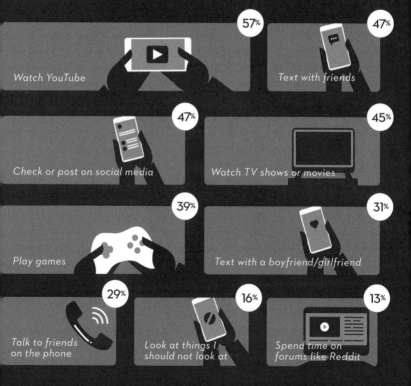

57% *Watch YouTube*

47% *Text with friends*

47% *Check or post on social media*

45% *Watch TV shows or movies*

39% *Play games*

31% *Text with a boyfriend/girlfriend*

29% *Talk to friends on the phone*

16% *Look at things I should not look at*

13% *Spend time on forums like Reddit*

n=1,154 teens and young adults ages 13–21 who own a cell phone or have access to a PC or tablet, June 26 to July 11, 2019.

5

we don't have
to edit our lives

lying online

My first memory of Facebook is from fifth-grade art class.

We were sitting in our little kids' chairs, arranging Perler beads into intricate designs, eagerly discussing the latest fifth-grade gossip. At that time, tech was the hottest topic there was. So one kid regaled us with tales of his new PlayStation, the greatest machine on earth. Another boasted of her architectural triumphs in Minecraft. But the moment that wowed everyone at the table was when a kid I'll call Tony, while perfecting his Perler bead robot, solemnly announced to us all, "I just got a Facebook."

This would be nothing to brag about now; thanks to our elderly relatives, Facebook is officially the least cool social media platform. But in my fifth-grade year, it was new and untarnished by our grandparents' laborious posts. Plus, we knew that it had an age restriction—thirteen and up—making it Very Cool in the eyes of a bunch of ten-year-olds.

Tony's brilliant discovery was that Facebook couldn't find out if you lied about your age. You could pick whatever age you wanted to be and log into a magical world.

The funny thing is, I don't remember what anyone did on Facebook. I didn't get (and still don't have) an account, so I have no idea what anyone posted. (I mean really, what is a fifth grader going to say? "Look at this cool Perler bead flower I made!" "Just learned about long division!")

But the power to shape yourself—the power to create an image of yourself and share it, even if you had to register that image as a thirteen-year-old—that was powerful. Even at age ten, my classmates loved the idea of social media, despite having to lie to start an account.

I don't know about you, but I'm not surprised that people enjoy the prospect of social media. It's a great idea! Keeping in touch with friends far away? Sharing the little moments you might forget about? Sign me up!

But I didn't have social media until high school. And when I looked at my friends on social media, I don't remember feeling envy but rather confusion. From the outside, it didn't seem fun.

What Forms of Social Media Do You Use Regularly?

■ 13-15 ■ 16-18 ■ 19-21

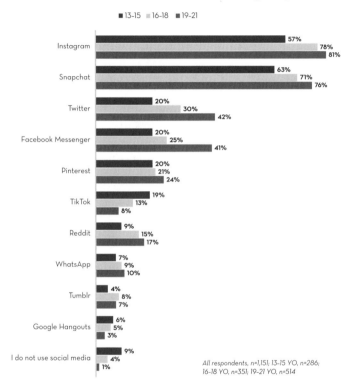

	13-15	16-18	19-21
Instagram	57%	78%	81%
Snapchat	63%	71%	76%
Twitter	20%	30%	42%
Facebook Messenger	20%	25%	41%
Pinterest	20%	21%	24%
TikTok	19%	13%	8%
Reddit	9%	15%	17%
WhatsApp	7%	9%	10%
Tumblr	4%	8%	7%
Google Hangouts	6%	5%	3%
I do not use social media	9%	4%	1%

All respondents, n=1,151; 13-15 YO, n=286; 16-18 YO, n=351; 19-21 YO, n=514

When my classmates started out on social media, it looked like a job to me. They went to desperate lengths to gain followers—one way was to scrawl your username on a whiteboard or a lunch table. They'd calculate the times of day they posted to maximize the number of likes; the difference between 190 and 200 likes was huge. It seemed stressful; social media presence was a new marker of status at our school. If your words weren't funny enough or your pictures artsy enough, you slid down the ladder.

I eventually started to use social media once I made friends who didn't live nearby, mostly from summer camps. In ninth grade I got Snapchat. I probably had twenty friends for the first year, and I didn't have any streaks for months, but I thought it was fun. Later, when I started an Instagram account, I just posted what I wanted to post. I had fewer than a hundred followers for a while, and I genuinely didn't care much about likes.

Honestly? It was great. It's exhilarating to keep in touch with friends from far away and share moments that make us smile. Nearly half of respondents (49 percent) in our survey agreed that they feel genuinely connected to people through social media.

At first, social media felt fulfilling.

But now, just a few years after I started on social media, it feels totally different. I laugh when I look back at those old posts, because I posted like an adult. Do you follow any adults on Instagram—maybe your youth pastor or an aunt or uncle? With all love to the over-eighteens of the world, their posting habits are nothing like ours. They'll post photos of a salad with a smiley face caption, or a coffee mug next to a book with an inspirational quote. Growing up certainly changes how you do social media!

That's how I posted at first, when I had just a few followers who were close friends. But naturally, as time passed, more people started to follow me. And a lot of them were people I didn't know as well—after all, nobody has hundreds of best friends.

The thing is, we all behave differently around our best friends than around that random kid at our table in math class. So as my follower count started to grow, I became less free on social media. My close friends would probably enjoy pictures of the cupcakes I'd made with my cousins. But other people might get annoyed. I know this because I've thought it myself. I see someone share a bit more than I'm interested in, and I think, *Why did this guy have to post this picture of his new pet rock? Literally nobody cares!*

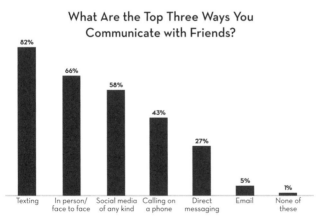

What Are the Top Three Ways You Communicate with Friends?

82%	66%	58%	43%	27%	5%	1%
Texting	In person/ face to face	Social media of any kind	Calling on a phone	Direct messaging	Email	None of these

All respondents, n=1,154

Once my social media account started to grow, I couldn't be very personal; I had to share at a shallower level. And, just as it had for my classmates in middle school, social media started to feel like work to me.

(Do you know that 86 percent of us reach for our phone first thing in the morning? Nearly the same number of us [80 percent] make it the last thing we do at night. And a hefty one third of us [32 percent] wake up in the middle of the night to check it. That sounds like work—or obsession—to me!)

So after an experiment with social media—and some fun along the way—I've found myself returning to my childhood habits. I haven't posted to Instagram in over a year, and I don't think I've started any new streaks for two years. Social media hasn't ruined my life, but it hasn't improved it much. I'm drifting back toward a life without it.

To be honest, I'm tempted to frame this as a noble decision: look how brave and wise I am, that I've chosen to set aside social media for my own good! Aren't you impressed?

But let's be real. I didn't do this because I'm special and smart. I did it because I'm human. And because I'm human, I care a whole lot about what other people think of me. Social media just made that an uncomfortably high priority.

Just because we're people, we all really, really care about what other people think of us. To be sure, not everyone wants everyone to like them. Some people only care about a few people's opinions. Some people don't care if others like or dislike them, just so long as other people care. Some people want everyone else to think they don't care.

In some ways, this is essential. If we truly didn't care what anyone thought—if we made a friend cry and didn't feel guilty, if we never took anyone's advice—we'd never have healthy relationships. We need to care.

But there's a huge difference between caring about *other people* and caring about what other people think of *us*.

When I worry about a kid in my math class thinking I'm dumb, or stress over what people will think when they hear me sing, I'm not caring for them. I'm thinking about myself. I'm stressed about the image I want to create of myself, fearful I'm not living up to it. I'm not trying to make the lives of *others* better—just my own.

This tricky paradox plays into our use of social media. Who's the center of attention on Instagram—other people or me? It's complicated. On the one hand, I'm constantly consuming images from other people, liking and commenting on their photos and not mine. On the other hand, everyone is focused on themselves. Their posts are not really messages directly to me, more like a peek into their diary (a published and thoroughly edited diary). And when I post, my thoughts about others are inextricably tied to thoughts about myself.

Obviously, my self-interest hasn't been fixed by just using social media less. But I do notice that social media brings out more of what's already inside me—a subtle belief that I am the center of the universe.

Honestly, the internet tends to make other people less peopley. When we see someone on the web, we're seeing a flattened, condensed version of them. We're seeing them in a bunch of pixels, a few comments they've posted.

When I'm immersed in technology, I'm the only person I see there. Hopefully I'm being vaguely reminded of the existence of others—but maybe not.

Sometimes this is necessary. When I text my mom to ask what groceries I need to pick up, it's not absolutely necessary for me to think through all the sacrifices she has made for me or the thrilling and important life she leads outside of my existence. I just need to know if we're out of milk.

However, if we spend a lot of time in the impersonal world of the internet, it can make us the only real person we're spending time with. And it's not great to be the center of our own universe.

Thinking too much about ourselves doesn't always look like arrogance. When I think of someone who's way too self-centered, I think of someone who thinks they're the greatest person in the world—someone who's convinced they're the most important person in every room. But you don't have to be stuck-up to be self-centered. Personally, I'm not too tempted to think I'm the best. I'm more tempted to think I'm the worst.

As I mentioned in the opening chapter, I've struggled with insecurity. I've allowed my own fears about who I am to influence how I behave around other people. I've spent whole conversations thinking all about myself: negative things about myself, yes, but all about me.

Social media encourages this kind of self-centeredness too. When I see friends having fun at the hockey game while I'm struggling with a homework assignment, I start thinking about myself. How unlucky I am, how I don't deserve to have this much work, how annoyed I am nobody asked *me* to go to the game. It sends me into a spiral that's all about me.

You know what? This is exhausting.

Because if we go into a social situation focused on *ourselves*—all the stupid things we might do, all the great things people might think of us—it ruins everything. With that kind of attitude, we can't relax and get to know everyone else.

To really enjoy life, we can't think about ourselves too much.

It's hard, for sure. But it's worth confronting the lies we tell ourselves. It feels good when we're not the most important one in the room.

• • •

I talked a lot in the last chapter about the ways tech helps us hide stuff. Unfortunately, social media helps us not just hide things we don't want others to see but also distort the truth of our lives. We get to make a whole new self. And while this is exhilarating for a day, it's exhausting for a lifetime.

The thing is, when we're surrounded by people telling us how great their lives are, we kind of want to be cool too. And social media is the premiere destination for talking about how great life is.

This makes a lot of sense—if we have five hundred followers, some of whom are real-life best friends and some of whom are just people we said hi to at a summer camp once, we only want to share the highlights. And it makes sense that we want to share them. We want to share what brings us joy.

However, spending hours and hours looking only at others' best moments, not seeing anything else, can take a real toll.

It so happened that last summer, when I was mostly just sitting at home writing this book, a lot of my friends were having, well, a lot more fun than me. My Instagram feed had a disproportionate number of pictures from France, Hawaii, or the Bahamas. I was mostly happy for these friends, but envy started to creep in: if only *I* was on vacation instead of wrestling with chapter titles and comma splices. Surely *I* deserved to get a glamorous vacation.

It spoiled my joy. Instead of being grateful for the incredible opportunity to write and enjoying my pleasant (and air-conditioned) home, I found myself frowning whenever I opened the app. Envy is a big enough problem that the Ten Commandments repeat it over and over: "You shall not covet your neighbor's house; you shall not covet your neighbor's wife, or his male servant, or his female servant, or his ox, or his donkey, or anything that is your neighbor's."[1] I'm probably not going to covet anyone else's donkey, but social media presents a real temptation to envy the money and the time and

In Search of Validation

(percent excludes those who say they don't use social media)

■ Strongly agree   ■ Somewhat agree   ■ Neither agree nor disagree
■ Somewhat disagree   ■ Strongly disagree

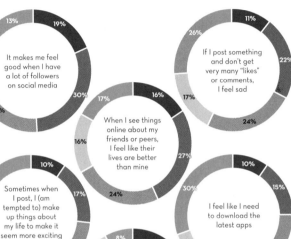

It makes me feel good when I have a lot of followers on social media
19% · 30% · 25% · 13% · 13%

If I post something and don't get very many "likes" or comments, I feel sad
11% · 22% · 24% · 17% · 26%

When I see things online about my friends or peers, I feel like their lives are better than mine
16% · 27% · 24% · 16% · 17%

Sometimes when I post, I (am tempted to) make up things about my life to make it seem more exciting or interesting
10% · 17% · 22% · 19% · 32%

I feel like I need to download the latest apps
10% · 15% · 22% · 23% · 30%

I feel genuinely connected to people through social media
18% · 31% · 27% · 15% · 8%

Sometimes it's exhausting to keep up with all the posts online
22% · 29% · 25% · 12% · 12%

I get bored easily when I'm not online
17% · 30% · 24% · 17% · 12%

Youth who use social media, n=1,102

the beauty of others, and I have to make the conscious choice to avoid its temptations.

I worry about how easy it is to spend hours and hours coveting.

Aren't we all aware of this, though? Of course our profiles are polished and perfected! We know they don't look like real life. And now it's trendy to share our imperfections—intentionally blurry photos, ironic captions alluding to how messy we really are. Doesn't that solve everything?

For sure, it's good to be aware of how curated our social media can be. And it helps to share our vulnerabilities and mistakes. But our social media profiles will always be shaped to give others a slice of our lives. I'm worried that this careful curating doesn't just affect what we share online but also how we live every day.

I've come to learn that the real highlights of life are often mundane. Last summer, I got to walk to my job pretty much every day, and it was gorgeous. In the early morning, the air wasn't hot but cool and fresh and clean-smelling. My neighbor's cat would rub against my legs, trying to distract me. Gold and pink clouds dotted the sky, and the morning sun sparkled on wet tree leaves.

These walks were moments of genuine joy and contentment; I felt at peace with myself and the world. They were highlights.

What if, one Tuesday, I'd tried to share my morning walk? Well, if I'd tried to photograph the sky, I'd have gotten a bunch of telephone wires and house roofs. If I'd tried to Snap the cat (a fluffy gray friend named Dragon), he would have skittered away as soon as I tried to capture his pose. I doubt I would have been able to come up with a joke about it. Our own joyful moments won't always entertain other people, and that's okay.

But by the standards of social media, it's not okay. Social media doesn't reward us for joy—it rewards us for entertainment. Our followers like or retweet us if we post amusing content with snappy captions and aesthetic lighting. I wouldn't get many likes on a blurry picture of the sky or a description of my simple walk, unless I'd spent hours thinking of how to make a joke out of my morning or a meme to pair with it. By the standards of my followers, that morning walk was useless.

If we let these standards rule our lives, we'll drown in insecurity. We can only have a healthy relationship with social media if we recognize that it doesn't govern our day-to-day lives, that dull lighting and poor framing don't erase life's worth. Yet we spend hours on social media; we immerse ourselves in its rules. We aren't immune to its lies.

Being tech-wise doesn't necessarily mean abandoning social media. But as I've started to figure out my relationship with technology, I've realized that I flourish most when sharing is a side effect, not a purpose. I feel happiest and most fulfilled when a good post isn't the goal of hanging out with friends or spending time with family but merely something that happens along the way.

What would it look like if we flipped the standards of social media? What if, when we had photogenic days, we let them be, not mentioning them on social media? What if we didn't share our accomplishments so broadly but spread them one-on-one with family and friends? Or, to look at it from the opposite direction, what if we posted things that didn't meet social media standards—a great dance with bad photos, or a fun summer camp with no clever quotes? Maybe our social media accounts would look different if we shared the boring highlights of our lives.

• • •

I wish I could say I'd started a grand experiment and began sharing real vulnerability with my Instagram followers. Truth is, I didn't. I went a different way and just stopped posting. I gave up. I didn't try to change the system.

You could. You could try to change the way you do social media, not just getting rid of it but really working within it.

How could you redeem it?

I can't give you specifics—as I say, I really haven't done that. But I've seen glimpses. One of my friends uses her Instagram exclusively to praise her friends. Every single post! One recent post was a birthday shout-out with a two-hundred-word caption, another a clip of her friend reaching the finish line at his track meet, another a concert. Similarly, a guy I know uses social media to post art and poetry he loves, a welcome break from the reels of highlights I'm scrolling through.

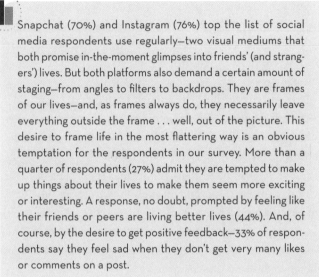

Snapchat (70%) and Instagram (76%) top the list of social media respondents use regularly—two visual mediums that both promise in-the-moment glimpses into friends' (and strangers') lives. But both platforms also demand a certain amount of staging—from angles to filters to backdrops. They are frames of our lives—and, as frames always do, they necessarily leave everything outside the frame . . . well, out of the picture. This desire to frame life in the most flattering way is an obvious temptation for the respondents in our survey. More than a quarter of respondents (27%) admit they are tempted to make up things about their lives to make them seem more exciting or interesting. A response, no doubt, prompted by feeling like their friends or peers are living better lives (44%). And, of course, by the desire to get positive feedback—33% of respondents say they feel sad when they don't get very many likes or comments on a post.

My friend Caroline chose to do a follower purge. After a summer full of FOMO and the pain of seeing everyone else's highlights, she decided she needed a change. After taking a social media break, she did a very thorough scrub of who she was following. The only people she kept following were those she would actually have a conversation with if she ran into them on the street. As she said to me, "What's the point of following people if you don't have a personal relationship with them?"

If you stick with it, make sure social media is just a part of your life—not the way you live life.

For me, this means going beyond what's easy. In real life and on the internet, I have several easy friendships. I say hi to the other person in class (easy), send a few texts from time to time (easy), like their profile pictures (literally just a flick of my fingers).

But to have the kind of friend who will give me a shoulder to cry on? That means I have to invest. That means I have to take on the hard task of vulnerability. I can't just like her photos; I have to show up for her at midnight.

In life, we will have many friendships that make us smile from day to day but aren't enough to wipe away our tears. But we also need a few friendships that go beyond this, those where we give up our own convenience for each other. This means that we need friendships where we take the hard way, where we show up in person.

What would it look like if instead of using social media to substitute for relationships, we used it as a springboard? If we used posts as an opportunity to spark conversations, to provide encouragement?

Honestly, I haven't done this. But maybe you could.

• • •

Social media isn't going away. And I'm going to be honest: right here and right now, it's causing us a lot of issues. More than four in ten respondents (43 percent) agreed that when they see things online about friends or peers, they feel like their friends' lives are better than their own.

It doesn't have to be this way.

Right now, social media is all about us. But what if we imagine for a moment that life isn't about us—and shouldn't be? Hierarchy wouldn't matter. We'd get to simply *be*, with no fears about how we'll be perceived.

How can we have this self-confidence and self-forgetfulness? My faith tells me it's through love—the love of God and of the ones we love. No matter whether or not you're above average in talent or appearance or wealth, being loved makes you important. The only way we can escape a hierarchy is to replace it with a loving community, a community based on mutual value.

Social media isn't much of a community right now, and sadly, many teens don't feel like they have one in real life. But maybe we could. Maybe we could be the change. Instead of cataloguing likes and comments, we could offer and receive the generosity of love.

- -

WHAT TO DO NEXT
Practices for Your Tech-Wise Life

» Think about your relationship with social media. Do you feel more connected when you use it? Do you feel happier when you use it? Are you honest when you use it?

» If you answer no to these questions, you might want to rethink your use of social media. Consider just getting rid of it! It's not as crazy as it sounds. I feel just as in touch with my friends as I did when I was using social media regularly. (Just make sure you mention to people that you won't be as reachable online.)

» Timothy hardly uses social media, but he—like all of us— wants to keep in touch with friends. So he intentionally checks in with friends through other methods. Instead of waiting to see what they post, he reaches out to see what's up. What would it look like for you to use social media to start conversations, not replace them?

» Try social media breaks. My friend Abby likes to download and delete her apps depending on her stress and busy- ness level. That way, she can happily enjoy social media when she has the time and emotional space, and it won't bother her when she's under stress.

» Use your social media to celebrate other people! Cel- ebrate the birthdays and milestones of your friends. It'll make you *and* them feel great.

» Stop and think before you take a photo, and stop and think again before posting it online. Will documenting and sharing help you to appreciate the moment or distract you and make you feel worse?

» Consider who you follow on social media. Do you like the thought of your followers getting to see your life, or does it make you nervous that you'll be judged? A purge might help—try Caroline's helpful rule.

Dear Amy,

I said in my last letter that this book isn't really about technology. I've been thinking about that a bit more, and this chapter helps me sort out my thoughts. In some ways, although this chapter is about social media, it's really about envy and pride and how we can get free of them. Envy and pride have been part of the messed-up human story for a long time. So why do they loom so large when we plunge into social media? And why do they seem somehow even more powerful there than in "real" life?

I think it has to do with the fundamental thing our society has asked technology to do. Its main function, I'm pretty sure, has always been to make life easier. "Easy everywhere" is what I called it in *The Tech-Wise Family*, and it's the basic promise technology makes. Buy this product, and something in your life will become easier and more available anywhere and everywhere you want it to be. That can be communication (the telephone, text messaging), information (the internet), or even just pleasant, cool air (central air conditioning). Easy everywhere is technology's goal.

The problem is that it's not just good things that technology makes easy and available everywhere. It also does the same with bad things.

There's a story in the Chronicles of Narnia series that we read when you were a kid, from *The Voyage of the Dawn Treader*. As you'll remember, the ship *Dawn Treader* visits a series of fantastical islands in search of the seven lost lords of Narnia. One of the islands they visit is especially strange because it's entirely covered by a gray cloud. As the adventurers approach, rowing toward the fringes of the cloud, they encounter a man frantically, desperately swimming away from the island. (He turns out to be one of the missing lords.) As they take him on board, he urges them, "Fly! Fly! . . . This is the island where dreams come true."

At first, rather than rowing the other direction, the adventurers think that sounds attractive.

> *"That's the island I've been looking for this long time,"* said one of the sailors. *"I reckoned I'd find I was married to Nancy if we landed here."*
>
> *"And I'd find Tom alive again,"* said another.
>
> *"Fools!"* said the man, stamping his foot with rage. *"That is the sort of talk that brought me here, and I'd better have been drowned or never born. Do you hear what I say? This is where dreams—dreams, do you understand—come to life, come real. Not daydreams: dreams."*[2]

And then, realizing that on this island every dream would come true—all their nightmares, all their worst fears, not just their happy daydreams—everyone on board begins rowing furiously in the other direction.

I think this is something like what has happened with technology. We heard that technology would give us easy everywhere and, just like you and your fifth-grade classmates hearing about "getting a Facebook," we were intrigued. Maybe here our dreams—of self-expression, of connection, maybe of fame and status and friendship—would come true.

But what we didn't realize is that technology, of all sorts, wouldn't just make our lives easier in good ways. It would also make them easier in all the worst ways.

Shame. Bullying. Competition. And, of course, envy and pride. All of them become easier, much easier, with technology. And because technology promises to follow us everywhere, they do too.

Meanwhile, the things that really make our lives better—the honesty and vulnerability you write about so beautifully here, the real highlights of our days—actually don't ever come easily. There's no way to make them easier, so there's nothing for technology to add. They come as gifts to those willing to wait, and sometimes to suffer. They aren't something we can just get with the push of a button.

So while technology is making many of the worst parts of our lives—the worst parts of ourselves—easier and, well, "everywherer," it can't do much to help make the best parts of our lives come true. Maybe technology has always been about our dreams—our fantasies about ourselves, our imagination of what an easy life could be like. But real life is not really like a dream. It's harder—there's certainly no "easy everywhere" in a real life—but it's far better as well.

Love,
Dad

6

we don't have to avoid boredom

bingeing entertainment

The last day of school is a triumph for everyone. Classes are emptier than usual, thanks to the lucky kids who are already on vacation or just decided it wasn't worth it; teachers are relaxed, handing back the last assignments they'll have to grade for a while; the bus ride home is loud and excited, with summer plans in the air. Everyone is ready for a break.

When I was really young, summertime was just rest and fun, full of playdates with friends and summer programs at the elementary school. (Keeping me busy was a chore for my parents, but that didn't occur to me.) As I grew older, summers had more structure; I'd either get a formal job (camp counseling, administrative work at the local college) or fill my days with babysitting, lawn mowing, and other odd jobs. My friends got jobs and vacationed too, so summer was far from the idyllic, no-responsibilities time of my childhood. Still, summer was much more flexible than the school year, with most of us working only part-time and unburdened by homework.

Shouldn't more free time mean more fun? No restrictions? Getting to do whatever you want? Sign me up.

But I started to notice something weird as I grew up. During the summers, as pleasant as it was to sleep in every day, somehow my classmates and I were all complaining of the same thing: boredom.

Not everyone, of course. And summer was still super fun. But while it was great not to be going to school every day, we had to figure out how we were going to spend all those free hours. Summers where I live are hot, humid, and full of thunderstorms; going outside (except to the pool) wasn't too appealing. I saw Snap stories with "HMU I'm bored" right alongside the ones bragging about glamorous vacations.

One easy solution was Netflix, so my friends all started barreling through season after season of TV. Video games were another option, for those who had PlayStations or XBoxes, and I learned to play Mario Kart during summer days spent at friends' houses.

We had all the free time in the world. We didn't have to do the schoolwork we complained about during the year.

But we were bored.

• • •

Now, I can't say I'm struggling right now with way too much free time. I bet it's not a typical problem for you, either. During the school year, it feels like free time is in short supply. And even during the summer, not everyone can work only part-time.

But boredom still pops up. During classes, while doing homework, while procrastinating, we itch to be doing something fun and exciting. And during moments of free time, we feel like there's nothing to do.

It's the worst feeling.

Now that most of us have tiny computers in our pockets, we'd think tech would be the perfect way to fix it. There's always something new to fill every spare moment—right?

But here's the problem I've noticed: when I try to distract myself with technology, I end up just as bored.

A few months ago, I deleted Instagram from my phone because it was pretty much a black hole for my time. Before I deleted it, it was my favorite cure for boredom—I'd mindlessly pull out my phone and stare at the hundreds of pictures my friends, acquaintances, and enemies had posted.

Did it work? Well, sort of. It did give me something to do. I'd look through the endless array of sports photos or beach pictures or selfies, double tapping if I liked one, smiling occasionally. And if I got to the end of the new photos, I'd just keep going and remind myself of what I'd already seen.

Yet I started to notice that this wasn't a cure for boredom. It was just a different *kind* of boredom. You see, as I scrolled, I would just get more and more bored. *Another* member of the soccer team posting an identical group pic? A whole album of ten different mirror poses? I'd keep scrolling—it was hard to stop—but I couldn't care less about what I was scrolling through. I wanted something new and thrilling, not a bunch of stale photos from people I didn't know that well.

I've noticed this problem with a lot of my boredom cures. I love to read the news on my phone—yes, you've figured out my secret, I'm actually a grandma—but I get bored after a few minutes. Why? Because I run out of anything that's actually new; the articles all blur into the same boring takes I've seen a million times. I keep scrolling and refreshing, hoping that something actually interesting will come along. (I know news is not what you might think of when you think procrastination. But it makes me feel smart and productive even when I actually have a million assignments to do, so it's a pretty clever way to waste time without feeling guilty about it.) Similarly, on the way to opening a new Google Doc, I'll open my favorite food blog and waste another hour staring at recipes and wishing the blogger would post something new.

After a few minutes on any of these time sucks, I run out of stuff I actually enjoy and have to be satisfied with reruns. Even when there's a new article or YouTube video or recipe, it feels the same. I get bored after thirty seconds of staring.

What Do You Spend Most of Your Time Doing When You Are Using an Electronic Device? Of These Activities, Which Three Do You Do the Most Often?

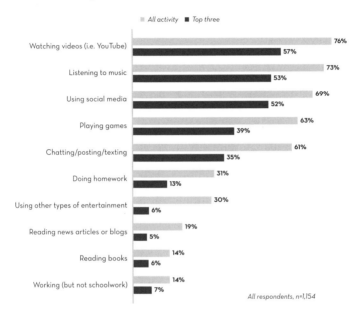

All respondents, n=1,154

Tech isn't as great at curing my boredom as it seems. So, how do we actually break free of boredom? How do we escape the dull distractions of our devices?

When I was growing up, dealing with boredom was actually pretty mundane. It happened during every car ride.

Like most parents with young kids, my mom and dad avoided going on long car rides with us whenever possible.

Have you ever gone on a car ride with kids? It's a slog. After two minutes, they'll start to whine that they're bored and the car is too hot and are they there yet?

But we lived in a pretty small town, so we had to take car rides to a lot of places—middle school, church, the grocery store, the mall. And when we went on vacation, it always meant a long, long car ride. So little Timothy and I had plenty of time to whine to our parents, and they had plenty of time to get exasperated with us. There's no worse place to be bored than a car, where you're literally strapped into a seat for hours on end.

What do you do with that time? Well, an easy way to spend it is through tech. It's better for us to be bored while staring at a screen than bored while screaming our heads off at Mom and Dad, right? It was probably tempting to them to give us their phones to look at or to get a tablet for us to play with or a DVD player for the car.

Well, that's not what they did. My brother and I didn't have phones or iPods as kids, and the car was a screen-free zone. I only remember one time when we were allowed to watch a movie—it was during a ten-hour drive to Maine, when even my parents decided it was worth it. (Ten hours with two elementary school children in a small car? Guaranteed to drive even the saintliest of moms and dads crazy.)

During those hours of car rides, we turned the boredom into something else. We played a lot of games from just what we saw around us; one favorite was to try to go through the alphabet using the words around us. A street sign reading "Baltimore

Pike" would give me *A*, and my brother would quickly yell "*B* too." When my mom then saw a "used cars" billboard, she'd triumphantly claim *C*. As you can imagine, some letters were a bit more challenging, but we learned to count on the Quality Inn on the highway for our *Q* or *Y*.

I also really liked to make up songs about whatever we were passing, which produced some musical masterpieces about cows. (Have you ever tried to write a song about a cow? I highly recommend it.)

But the day that changed our car rides forever was when I read aloud from a book of my grandpa's that was full of puzzles and riddles. Silly things: "There were seven apples in a basket and seven girls in the room. Each girl took one apple, but one apple remained in the basket. How?"[1]

Now, we quickly grew good at guessing the real answers. But half the fun was making up even more ridiculous possible answers: maybe one of the girls *was* the basket! Maybe a rogue mouse had brought in an extra apple!

Now that Timothy and I are at least slightly more grown up, we don't usually play games or tell riddles. Instead, our car times are usually full of conversation or looking around at where we're driving. (I like spotting unusual features along the road—I recently noticed a knitting shop called "The Sated Sheep," which might be the weirdest store name I've ever seen.) Or we listen to music as a family—no headphones in the car!

Unfortunately, now that we have smartphones, it's all too easy for a notification to buzz and one of us to pull out a phone and glance at it, effectively killing whatever conversation was happening beforehand. I don't like this; I've learned that our times in the car are way better than whatever is buzzing my phone.

So I like to get my phone out of the way or leave it behind if possible. For instance, when we go to church, which is a thirty-minute drive away, I don't need my phone. I just leave it at home, and we're forced to have a family discussion. Or if I absolutely have to have it, I put it far away. Buried in a backpack, or way out of arm's reach.

Of course, by avoiding my phone, I'm opening myself to the possibility of boredom. Yet it's only by accepting the possibility of a little boredom that I'm open to the much more exciting possibilities—spotting a "Buy One Get Five Free" sign for fireworks or hearing a hilarious joke from my brother.

I think my childhood car rides offer a few clues to how we can mitigate boredom. First of all, we have to accept a little of it. Remember the "seven-minute rule" of conversation I talked about earlier? Honestly, it takes a few minutes before you figure out something fun to do or sink into the fun you're having.

And the other clue: the cure for boredom isn't always adding something but paying closer attention to what's already there. Who would have thought that billboards could entertain us for hours? But Timothy and I were enthralled just by looking at the letters that were already passing us by.

What really helps boredom is diving deeper into the world around us. I worked on a ranch a few summers ago, and I did pretty repetitive work: pulling out weeds, staining signs, raking brush. But it wasn't boring; it was thrilling. I loved clearing patches of garden for the plants, even when the thorny weeds scratched my arms. I loved feeling a rare breeze through my sweaty hair as I raked up piles and piles of branches and grass. I laughed every time I fed the pigs (heartlessly named Pork and Chop) and saw them fighting over watermelon rinds. And I shivered with joy when I'd pause in my work, look up, and see a blue, blue sky.

The cure for boredom is not distraction. It's wonder.

The poet Gerard Manley Hopkins wrote, "The world is charged with the grandeur of God."[2] Think about what that means. Think about what it means for every leaf and rock to be alive, charged, sparking—that's what wonder is, when we see suddenly that something mundane has God hidden in it.

Unfortunately, technology doesn't always encourage wonder in us. Sometimes it does! TV shows and movies can spark contemplation and appreciation. The internet can give us incredible glimpses of places and people we'd never see in our own little worlds; I'll never forget watching a documentary about ducks with two of my cousins (duck-umentary?) and our jaws dropping as tiny ducklings plunged forty feet through the air from a tree, landing safely in a pile of leaves. And our amazing technological resources for communication can help us to love those around us much more truly and kindly.

But this isn't really the default. I fear that the default mode of our devices is to compress the world into flat images and quick takes, replacing wonder with mere distraction.

Take video games. In the few decades since video games were invented, they've taken over the social life of our generation, and we can see why—it's magical to be immersed into a brand-new world. Video games are pretty much the most absorbing way to entertain ourselves we've ever invented. The graphics are getting more and more gorgeous, with whole teams of artists crafting worlds for us to lose ourselves in. And in multiplayer games, our cool online personas get to interact with other people's cool online personas. Games are like TV, but we get to participate. There's nothing so enthralling.

Yet I think we need to consider carefully how it can affect us to immerse ourselves in such content. If we spend too much time in virtual worlds, our sense of wonder may be in danger.

Remember this from when we talked about social media? In general, we rarely use our devices to mirror the slow, painstaking parts of being human. To keep us engaged, all our tech aims to give us a mini dopamine rush whenever we do anything, whether that's opening a Snap, unlocking our phones, or collecting an in-game reward. In something like a video game, every second—literally every single frame!—is engineered to make us keep playing.

But our world isn't like this. Our lives are chock-full of boredom. The majesty of a mountain climb or an incredible conversation is amazing precisely *because* it's not an everyday experience. If we want to be satisfied in the world, we can't expect constant dopamine rushes; indeed, we need to be willing and able to pay attention to our lives, looking out for the moments that will inspire joy. Wonder won't always announce that it's coming. We need to be on a detective hunt for it.

If we spend too much time immersed in the most diverting entertainment in the world, how can we be pleased with the humdrum reality of life? In a video game, we don't *need* to pay attention to find something exciting. In everyday life, we do.

And the kind of never-ending interest of video games quickly becomes addictive. Why would we ever stop playing something, or watching something, that promises constant entertainment and infinite novelty?

My brother, Timothy, was uncomfortably reminded of tech's all-absorbing powers one Tuesday night in college. He had a long, drawn-out dinner with his roommate and a group of their friends, and they all got sucked into a riveting conversation, the kind where you let your food go cold on your plate and forget to go back for dessert. Eventually, people drifted away to study for upcoming exams and finish problem sets, and the conversation wound to a close.

Timothy and his roommate headed back to their room. They each settled into their desks, about six feet apart. His roommate pulled up Netflix, so Timothy looked for something to do too. He pulled up a game he'd downloaded a few days ago, a space adventure a friend had told him about, and started playing. Soon his roommate pulled out a box of Honey Nut Cheerios from a hidden drawer. He passed the Cheerios to Timothy. Timothy passed them back. And again. Hardly any words, mostly just Cheerio-filled grunts.

Episodes of *House of Cards* droned by. Timothy explored more and more virtual space, completing quest after quest. Suddenly, it was 1:30 am on a Tuesday night—no, Wednesday morning. They looked at each other and groaned.

Timothy still remembers how gross he felt—brain fried, back cramped, eyes blurry. And here's the thing: those hours of dinner conversation left him feeling joyful and refreshed. Those hours of video games left him feeling exhausted. But even as he started to feel worse and worse, he kept playing. On and on.

Tech can suck us in and pull our lives off balance. In fact, more than a quarter of people in our survey (27 percent) said one of the top challenges they face is balancing physical activity with online activity.

If we get used to the fast-paced entertainment that tech offers us, we'll end up sick. Think of the pain in your stomach when you've consumed too much soda or cake. While

The Top Three Challenges You Face When It Comes to Tech

Having a harder time focusing

38%

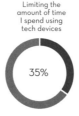

Limiting the amount of time I spend using tech devices

35%

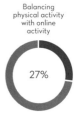

Balancing physical activity with online activity

27%

All respondents, n=1,154

entertainment isn't going to kill us, too much of it may dull us to the world around us—and just make us feel gross.

What brings lasting happiness? In my experience, happiness is more acute and long-lasting when it requires patience. I enjoy a nature documentary as much as any lover of the outdoors, but even the best documentary can't make me feel what I do when I reach the top of a mountain in time for a chilly sunrise. Real happiness takes time. Friendships grow through small jokes and shared connections, not all at once. It takes long labor to canoe to the middle of a lake. But these joys don't make us sick.

And there's wonder to be found no matter how prosaic the world might seem. Timothy doesn't share my passion for flowers, but he loves playing the viola and driving in his tiny white car. My cousin Dylan enjoys cliff jumping. And my friend Carley finds infinite wonder in clouds, texting me whenever she sees an unusual one.

If the world is boring, we can be patient. Remember the seven-minute rule? Engaging with the people around us may not begin with wonder; it may begin with awkwardness and boredom and a loss for words. Or it might float on the surface, as we hesitate to expose our humanity.

But reaching beyond the seven-minute point yields wonder we couldn't have imagined, not even in a video game. We have to learn to live with the boredom of our lives if we want to experience it.

• • •

Let's choose to pause before we turn on the TV or scroll through Instagram. Let's choose to live lives of attention, engaging with our world rather than closing our eyes to it. We don't need to abandon the fun that tech can give us; sometimes a night watching *Parks and Rec* is exactly what I need. But it's so easy to forget the things we love, so easy to believe that boredom is inevitable. It's so easy to reach for nearby devices to content ourselves with a different kind of boredom.

Honestly, we might need some pretty strong reminders at times. I have a whole list in my journal of Things to Do When I'm Bored: reading books, going for bike rides, baking cakes, making art. We need to pay attention to the things that really make us say "Wow!" and not forget what we love when we're in the doldrums of boredom.

Instead of staring glassy-eyed at screens, let's use our devices to wake up more. Let's watch shows and share delights with other people. Let's come together over screens, not slip apart.

This might take a little more work. It's worth it. Because of all the things we encounter in day-to-day life and work, wonder is what we carry with us.

My memories of school summers, those months of free time that both bored and thrilled us, are not of whatever technology I consumed. Rather, the memories that have stayed with me are memories of wonder.

I remember the books. I'd go to the public library every two weeks and pick out ten books—five nonfiction, five

The top three activities respondents do most often outside of school and sleep are watching videos (44%), listening to music (42%), and using social media (41%). What do these all have in common? Technology. Contrast this with the non-tech activities surveyed: doing homework (10%), working (5%), reading books (5%), and reading news (3%). We are spending a lot of our lives looking at screens! This might explain why two of the top three challenges respondents face when it comes to tech are about trying to get off tech: limiting the amount of time they spend using tech devices (35%) and balancing physical activity with online activity (27%).

fiction—and march back home with my heavy load. My parents would find me the books they'd loved when they were my age and many they still loved. I'd immerse myself in worlds both fantastical and historical, and I'd learn more about my own world. One summer I went on a biography kick, and I discovered the lives of many fascinating people: Marie Curie, Nelson Mandela, and my favorite, "Shark Lady" Eugenie Clark. During these summers, I tackled long, dense books that I'd never have time for during the school year, spending hours and hours in the big brown chair in our living room. They made me laugh and sob and think, and I'd come out of every good book with a small heartbreak that it had ended. Without moving me physically from the chair, these books moved me to wonder.

I also remember exploring. Lancaster County, largely peopled by the Pennsylvania Dutch community of Amish, was about fifty miles away. Because the Amish don't drive cars, Lancaster County is a perfect place to go on long bike rides; virtually the only traffic is slow-moving buggies with horses whose clip-clop can be heard from far away. My family would wake up early on a Saturday and head out to Lancaster for bike rides. We'd go up and down the rolling hills and marvel at the small farms with German names and laundry flapping on clotheslines. We'd bike next to small fields of corn and wheat and beans waving in the wind, on covered bridges over gleaming rivers, by small herds of fluffy sheep. And halfway through our ride, we'd stop at a small dairy farm for their freshly churned ice cream. I'd get caramel ice cream in a waffle cone and head over to see the cows whose milk had gone into the ice cream; they sat peacefully with their calves in pleasant stalls while barn cats sauntered by. This, too, was wonder.

And I remember serving. For seven summers, I went with my church youth group to help a local church that provided free home repair to the houses of its neighbors. I learned how to hang drywall, tar a roof, and use a power saw, and I spent a lot of time washing floors and painting and dusting. I got to know the owners of the houses I worked on; we chatted about everything from garden pests to the power of prayer. My friends and I sang as we worked, trying in vain to remember all the verses of songs we thought we knew well. We prayed with men and women we might never meet again. We gave blessing, and we received it.

Tech promised to distract me from my boredom. But it was these simple activities that took me beyond distraction. I didn't need my phone to escape, because the tech-wise life plunged me deep into wonder.

WHAT TO DO NEXT
Practices for Your Tech-Wise Life

» Think about the times you're bored. Is it usually while doing something that annoys you, like sitting through a boring class? Or is it during free time, when you don't really know what to do with yourself?

» Timothy likes to see boredom as an opportunity for creativity and joy. Wherever he goes, he tries to take a physical book along with him—that way, he always has something he can sink into rather than surf on top of.

» When you're bored, tech won't be a permanent solution. Instead of turning right to your phone when you're in a boring situation, try giving it a few minutes. Sit on the bus or in class without distraction; let a conversation unfold. Just a few minutes could be the time it takes to find something interesting.

» Make sure your favorite activities are accessible. It can feel like so much work to do the tiniest things when you're bored. If you love art, fill a desk drawer with art supplies. If you like to read, keep books everywhere you keep your tech—in your bedroom, living room, and kitchen. If you like to play sports, keep your equipment easily organized so you can start having fun right away. If you like to make music, put your instruments somewhere you'll see them all the time and be encouraged to pick them up.

. . . .

Dear Amy,

Even though I've said that this book isn't really about technology, this chapter is truly one that could only be written in the modern world. Because boredom really is a new thing in human history.

As I wrote in *The Tech-Wise Family*, there literally was no word for boredom in the English language before 1853 (the date it was first used in print, according to *Merriam-Webster*). There weren't words in other European languages for it either. It simply wasn't a concept for most of history. There is a somewhat related ancient idea, one of the seven deadly sins, called sloth or acedia, but it's not the same as our modern idea of aimless, restless boredom.

I think that's because all human beings used to live immersed in the difficult, dangerous, glorious natural world. We had to work hard, from daybreak to evening, and then for long hours we would sit and sleep under the unimaginably vast canopy of stars in the millennia before artificial light. Life wasn't easy, but it wasn't boring either.

So how did life become boring? Well, there's a story there as well. When the word started to be used in the nineteenth century, it was initially used almost entirely by the leisure classes—the rich who had almost literally all the work in their lives done by servants, from cooking to gardening and even to getting themselves dressed in the morning! They were the first to complain, sitting in their parlors or at lavish dinner tables, that the person next to them was a "bore."

And because so many of us now live with amazing amounts of leisure and free time, and with so little requirement to do really hard work in the midst of nature, we now get to experience the same boredom that was once the, um, privilege of the wealthy.

I have a friend, Steve Dubbeldam, who runs a company called Wilderness Collective. He leads expeditions down to the bottom of the Grand Canyon and into remote parts of the wilderness all over the United States. One of the amazing things about our country is how much wilderness is actually left, even though most of us live in cities and suburbs where we can barely see a dozen stars in the sky. Steve's company helps people get to those places together. The first thing he does at the beginning of a trip is take everyone's phone and lock it in a vault. (Not that phones work where they're going anyway!) People come back from Steve's trips with bruises, and sometimes broken bones; they come back incredibly tired. None of them ever come back and say they were bored.

Boredom is a problem that the modern world created and then tries to solve with more technology. But as you've discovered, technology somehow makes our boredom worse even as it serves up an endless series of distractions. I'm pretty sure, actually, that the more distracted we are, the more bored, and bore-able, we become.

I love that during some of your long school-free summers, you had enough free time to get bored. I'm worried that we parents try to solve the problem of boredom too quickly. We help you fill up your days with activities when it might be better just to make space to feel bored for a little while. Because, as you've discovered, creativity and wonder actually lie on the other side of boredom. It's when we're willing to put up with that gnawing restless sense that there's nothing to do—and not relieve it with a glowing rectangle—that we discover there actually is something worth doing and often people waiting to do something with us.

So, I guess I am adding this to the unlikely things I pray for you: that you'll have little enough busyness and distraction in your life that you'll experience just enough boredom. Because I'm pretty sure that on the other side of boredom you'll find something wonderful.

Love,
Dad

HOW OFTEN WOULD YOU SAY YOUR PARENTS/GUARDIANS TALK ABOUT...

	Daily	Weekly	Monthly	Less Often	Never
FORGIVENESS	24%	19%	23%	20%	14%
PATIENCE	29%	27%	18%	16%	11%
SELF-CONTROL	29%	23%	17%	18%	12%
WORK ETHIC/ DOING YOUR BEST	42%	28%	17%	8%	5%
RELIABILITY	28%	25%	22%	14%	11%
FAIRNESS	25%	23%	21%	17%	14%
BEING A GOOD FRIEND	25%	20%	22%	19%	15%
SERVING OTHERS	21%	22%	22%	18%	17%
SEX	5%	8%	14%	36%	37%
USING DEVICES WISELY	33%	22%	19%	15%	11%

n≈1,154 teens and young adults ages 13–21 who own a cell phone or have access to a PC or tablet, June 26 to July 11, 2019.

DO YOUR PARENTS/GUARDIANS HAVE ANY RULES ABOUT . . .

NO RULES   VERY FLEXIBLE RULES   SOMEWHAT FLEXIBLE RULES
SOMEWHAT STRICT RULES   VERY STRICT RULES

The kinds of apps you can download
52% 19% 16% 9% 4%

The kinds of online video games you can play
55% 18% 16% 8% 3%

The amount of time you can spend watching shows or movies
49% 21% 16% 9% 5%

The kinds of TV shows or movies you can watch
42% 20% 18% 12% 8%

Who you can text or chat with on your phone
49% 17% 16% 10% 8%

What you can look at on your phone
44% 15% 16% 15% 10%

HOW DO YOU FEEL ABOUT THESE RULES?

11% They are too strict   **83%** They are about right   **6%** They are too lenient

59% Most of the time   **27%** Some of the time   **11%** Not very often   **3%** Never

HOW OFTEN DO YOU FOLLOW THESE RULES?

teens and young adults ages 13–21 with a cell phone or table whose parents set rules for them on media consumption and content, June 26 to July 11, 2019.

7

we don't have
to be exhausted

when screens replace sleep

I f you ever have a conversation with me (which I hope you
do!), you'll learn something about me right away: I love
sleep. Like, *seriously* love it. Even if I have a final exam the
next day or a once-in-a-lifetime party to go to, I'm constantly
checking the clock to make sure I can get my eight hours in.
Yep, I said eight hours. I don't know how people survive on
four or five hours a night. I wake up cranky if I only get seven
and a half.

Now, you might not be as obsessed with sleep as I am. You
might even resent the fact that you have to sleep at all. But I
bet sleep affects your life whether you want it to or not. I've

noticed that when I ask my friends how they are, sleep is often the first thing they think of. They respond, "Ugh, not great. I'm so tired," or (rarely) "Honestly, awesome! I actually got some sleep last night!" Sleep makes a difference.

In fact, it plays an enormous role in our health and well-being—even though we're not conscious! Everyone knows the feeling of struggling through work after a short night of sleep, fighting against the urge to collapse for a nap. But losing sleep does more than make us cranky and tired; just one hour of lost sleep is associated with up to a 60 percent increase in symptoms of depression and anxiety among teenagers, so much so that sleep's effect on mental wellness "is likely larger than [that of] most therapies and medications."[1]

Sleep makes our habits, bodies, and minds healthier. In fact, sleep is productive. It might not seem like we're doing much when we go to bed, but our bodies actually take those hours to self-repair after a day's work. The National Sleep Foundation tells us that "sleep is an active period in which a lot of important processing, restoration, and strengthening occurs," despite how inactive it seems.[2] Isn't that cool? Our bodies repair themselves when we aren't even awake!

Unfortunately, we don't get enough of it. A poster in my high school nurse's office proclaimed that teens need nine hours of sleep to function, but just the words "nine hours of sleep" are enough to make any high schooler roll their eyes. How do you expect us to get that much sleep? Right after school, a lot of us are rushing about to sports practice or drama rehearsals or work or to babysit a sibling, and we barely have time to get homework done after that. And many of us have school days that start at 7:00 or 7:30. It's a frustrating choice: skip homework and get bad grades but a good night's sleep, or swallow some coffee and work late into the night?

You won't be surprised that I choose sleep every time.

I know exactly where I got my love of sleep: my mom and dad. My dad goes to bed as soon as he possibly can, and he takes a nap pretty much every day of his life. My mom is less of a napper, but she is devoted to the health benefits of sleep; whenever I get even slightly sick, her first solution is to tell me to skip all my responsibilities and go to bed. For my parents, sleep deprivation is pretty much a sickness in itself, and they wrote many absence notes to my school on days when I was exhausted and needed to rest. Sleep is the answer to all our ills in the Crouch family, and while unfortunately my mom and dad can't just send an absence note to work when they're feeling sleepy, they wanted me to learn to prioritize it when I can.

And beyond just sleep, my parents have always encouraged me to take care of myself and allow myself to rest. It's so easy to forget about our own well-being when we're rushing from school to cross-country practice to orchestra rehearsal, and my parents constantly reminded me that busyness and exhaustion get in the way of actually doing the activities we love.

It's no surprise, then, that my parents set a lot of boundaries around screens and rest. Why? Technology is a huge issue

Is There a Certain Time in the Evening after Which You Are Not Supposed to Use Your Phone or Other Devices?

■ Yes, every night   ■ Yes, but mainly just on weeknights   ■ No

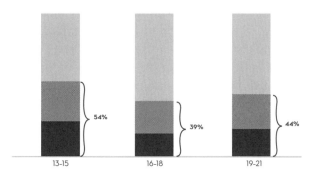

All respondents, n=1,154; 13-15 YO, n=289; 16-18 YO, n=351; 19-21 YO, n=514

when we're trying to sleep well. As always, technology isn't the source of these problems, but it sure makes them worse. On the work side of things, email and text and Google Docs have made it possible for us to be constantly accessible and constantly watched. My high school started using Google Docs pretty aggressively in my sophomore year, and my teachers could see if I wrote that paper in an hour or if I stayed up until 3:00 am or if I finished it a week before the deadline (I wish). Even if your school hasn't gone that far yet, the other kids in a group project can still bombard you with texts or passive-aggressive comments at any time of night.

Plus, technology's distracting powers make work take so much longer. While we're working, we flip through tabs, open

Do You Usually Sleep with Your Phone in Your Bedroom?

■ Yes ■ No

12%

88%

All respondents, n=1,154

Do You Currently Have a TV in Your Bedroom?

■ Yes ■ No

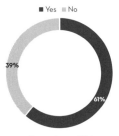

39%

61%

All respondents, n=1,154

notifications, and scroll through feeds, turning simple ten-minute jobs into hour-long tasks. Even worse, when we try to rest, our phones and computers take over too. After hours of homework, Netflix and YouTube promise an easy way to just turn our brain off and relax. Video games seem like a perfect way to let off some steam.

But here's the funny thing: often those "relaxing" activities actually get in the way of real rest. We stay up hours and hours into the night bingeing on TV shows; when one part of our brain says *Hey, maybe we should go to sleep*, another part says *Just one more episode.* Or we procrastinate for hours online and then realize it's 10:00 pm and the lab report is still due tomorrow. Or we climb into bed but see a text from someone and stay awake for another three hours chatting. Tech has a real effect on our sleeping habits; researchers found that "access to social media and especially a cell phone in teenagers' bedrooms is associated with a reduction in sleep time during the school week with negative effects on daily functioning and mood which increases with increasing age."[3] Yikes.

Let me tell you something important about myself: If I don't get enough sleep, my brain is little better than a decapitated slug. This means that my parents, preferring to have their daughter around rather than a delirious zombie, were pretty strict about getting me to sleep when I was a kid. And when technology started to enter my life, they quickly developed some firm principles around sleep and tech.

Their best rule was also their simplest. How do you keep your phone from distracting you when you sleep? Maybe just don't have it nearby when you sleep.

I got a taste of how much my parents were willing to enforce that rule when I got an iPod Touch in eighth grade. Up until this point, my mom had always woken me up in the morning, but this struck me as juvenile—hardly befitting of a grown-up person such as myself. A few days after I got the iPod, I had the delightful idea that I could use it as an alarm clock in the morning—I could wake up to chiming bells! Or chirping birds! Or quacking ducks!

"Mom," I said, "I can just use my iPod as an alarm. I'll wake up on my own!"

She frowned. I could see the disapproval creeping in. "I don't want you staying up looking at it."

"I won't," I said—and I really believed I wouldn't.

"Hmmm," she said.

"It has such nice alarm sounds! Listen!" I showed her the variety of alarms that could wake me up.

She still looked skeptical. "Hmm," she said again. "Maybe you could turn off the Wi-Fi when you go to sleep at night."

"Okay, sure."

But as she considered, she didn't seem totally happy with this plan. Then an idea came to her, and I saw triumph on her face. "I know!" she said. "We'll just buy you an alarm clock!"

And she did. Pretty soon, my parents presented me with a new alarm clock and my iPod stayed downstairs at night.

Guess what? This wasn't a dumb parental rule I wriggled out of as soon as possible. In fact, five or six years after that conversation, I *still* keep my phone out of my room at night.

Honestly, I feel a little sheepish about how much I need this discipline. Most nights, I plug my phone into an outlet in our kitchen and head upstairs to bed without a backward glance. But from time to time, my phone ends up in my room when I'm going to bed, and I yawn and think, *I can handle this.*

But you know what? I can't. You'd think I could just put it down and go to sleep. No way. Without fail, every single time I have my phone next to me at bedtime, I use it. Better just check that I don't have any texts, right? And then I should respond to those. And then, ooh, I should watch that video my friend sent me!

And then I look at the clock and see: whoops, I've spent half an hour flicking through my phone. A whole half hour that I could have been sleeping.

After Hours

How often do you do any of the following in your bedroom at night?

Text with friends

Check or post on social media

Watch YouTube

Spend time on forums like Reddit

Talk to friends on the phone

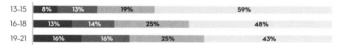

Text with a boyfriend/girlfriend

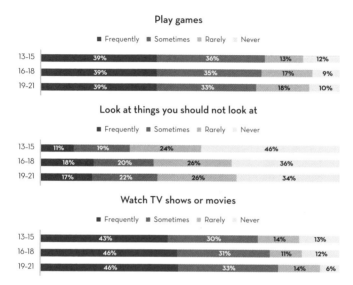

All respondents, n=1,154; 13–15 YO, n=289; 16–18 YO, n=351; 19–21 YO, n=514

And I think you know by now that I need that half hour of sleep.

• • •

Yet as marvelous as sleep is, it can't solve all our problems. What do we do about the exhaustion of our minds? How do we heal when our souls are weary?

Sleep alone won't heal us when we feel bruised and battered by the world. For that, we need something more.

Think of the things you love to do. Think of the things you'll never get tired of, no matter how often you do them. Think of the things that leave you full to the brim with happiness, maybe even spilling over.

For me, a good bike ride through my beautiful town, eating salted caramel ice cream with my friends, and spending time with a really fabulous book all leave me feeling not just happy but *restored*, like all the pieces of me have come together.

This is the kind of rest we need. To recover from our weary days, we need more than sleep; we need this soul-filling, heart-stirring, invigorating rest. And to find it, my family took on one of our hardest—and most rewarding—practices.

It's called *Sabbath*.

Since I was little, my family has kept this ancient Jewish tradition. The Sabbath (also called Shabbat or Shabbos) is the practice of setting aside one day each week for rest, and its origin is in the Hebrew Scriptures.

The fundamental law is from the Ten Commandments:

> Remember the Sabbath day, to keep it holy. Six days you shall labor, and do all your work, but the seventh day is a Sabbath to the LORD your God. On it you shall not do any work. . . . For in six days the LORD made heaven and earth, the sea, and all that is in them, and rested on the seventh day. Therefore the LORD blessed the Sabbath day and made it holy.[4]

This is *wild*. God is saying that taking a day off every week isn't lazy but divine. It's something we can—and should—do.

It's a day for worshiping and rejoicing—a day to let the world go on without us. Christians have few regulations for the Sabbath, but I try to take my example from God. If he rested on the seventh day of creation, I should too.

Don't misunderstand: Sabbath isn't a day where all fun is banished. If we overlegislate the Sabbath, we'll get no more rest than if we skipped it. We do follow some guidelines, but the essence of the Sabbath is joy—joy in God's presence, joy in our own gifts.

Every seventh day, my family imperfectly, haltingly practiced Sabbath. Let me tell you: Sabbath is not easy. Resting is not easy. Homework takes longer than expected and then comes rehearsal or sports practice Friday and friends want to hang out. Every Saturday, my mom or dad would ask me how I planned to finish my work before Sunday, and I didn't always have an answer. We had many, many Sabbaths that ended early so we could finish up pressing work.

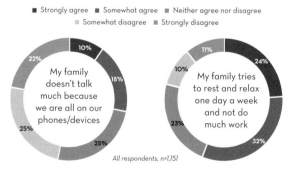

■ Strongly agree ■ Somewhat agree ■ Neither agree nor disagree
■ Somewhat disagree ■ Strongly disagree

My family doesn't talk much because we are all on our phones/devices
10%
22%
18%
25%
25%

My family tries to rest and relax one day a week and not do much work
11%
24%
10%
23%
32%

All respondents, n=1,151

Yet our failures fade beside the treasure I've received from our successes. To this day, I look forward to every Sunday morning, knowing that I will choose not to work, that I've prepared for it. That I've shaped my time so that on this beautiful Sunday, I will be able to rest and relax and rejoice.

On Sundays I like to have pancakes in the morning and read a book until it's time for church. Coming back from church, I frequently plan to go for a walk (although I often end up distracted by our neighborhood cats). Sometimes I take a nap; sometimes I work out. Sometimes I spend time with friends; sometimes I spend time by myself. At the end of the day, I go to sleep feeling ready for the week to come, fully prepared for the Monday that is to follow.

Now, you might be thinking, *Okay, Amy, I guess this sounds nice. But what does this have to do with technology?*

Our family Sabbaths are Sabbaths from screens. We don't give up screens completely—sometimes we watch a movie together in the evening—but we set them aside. I like to keep my phone plugged in at our kitchen counter all day. I'll open it if I see a message, but it stays parked there. And I don't usually need a laptop because I'm not working.

Why avoid tech on the Sabbath? It's not because it's ruining our lives. That's not the point of the Sabbath. We also give up work on the Sabbath, but work isn't wrong; it's essential to our lives and a beautiful way we can live out our purpose. In taking Sabbath, we don't condemn work but set it aside.

Similarly, technology isn't a Bad Thing. It's a tool that can be used well. Yet, like work, it easily creeps into more of our lives than we like, perhaps causing its own kind of exhaustion, stress, and difficulty.

Technology is also something we try to quit, over and over again. Sociologist Donna Freitas's survey of college students found that a majority of students had tried to quit social media, and many more had tried to curb their usage of it.[5] But it's hard to keep away from it for long—how would we function without our screens?

Just like work, technology is an important part of our lives that can easily take over. That's what Sabbath is for. By stepping back, we gain perspective over what's in charge of our lives—and whether we're comfortable with that.

● ● ●

What about the power of screens to help us relax? Dealing with our devices can be stressful, but they also promise us R&R. However, our devices might not be giving us the kind of rest we need. The Sabbath is meant to be like sleep—a time when we restore and repair and heal ourselves. Eight hours lying in bed and staring at the ceiling, while it looks something like sleep, won't give the benefits of true sleep. Similarly, many of the distractions of tech may *look* like relaxation but don't actually restore us much. Sabbath is meant to revitalize us—to re-life us.

I'm sure you've felt the slow, deadening feeling of having spent two hours on Facebook and feeling no better about life, or guilty exhaustion after hours of Netflix late at night. Remember how I talked about distraction way back at the beginning of this book? Technology is really good at distracting us, but it's not great at restoring us.

We also talked in the last chapter about engaging our minds in entertainment. The same principle applies with rest: we're most restored when we're engaged with our rest. When I'm watching one-minute cookie decorating videos on Instagram, I'm pretty passive. I stare at my screen, bored out of my mind, not thinking or caring much about what I see.

But other kinds of activities pull me in and make me relate to the world around me. My brother, Timothy, for instance, is always my movie buddy. Timothy is the kind of person who will happily spend three hours telling you about the latest movie he saw, and he's often disappointed that I don't keep up with film releases. So when we get to spend time together, we love to take that time to enjoy a movie.

A couple months ago, he was appalled to hear how few Marvel movies I'd seen, so on our next free evening, we popped popcorn, brewed some lemon tea (for me) and coffee (for him), and watched *Captain America: The Winter Soldier*. We oohed and aahed together over the fight scenes and held our breath as the plot unfolded. And as soon as the credits started to roll, we plunged into a fevered discussion about the whole thing that lasted for at least an hour. By watching a movie with my brother, I wasn't being distracted or distanced from him; I got to see him for more of who he is.

My family Sabbaths aren't about rules. They're about resting in mindful ways. They're about moving closer to the people and places we love.

• • •

I know Sabbath might seem absurd; it seems like a ridiculous sacrifice of time to give up an entire day to just do nothing. And on Saturday afternoons, I often grouse about how much more time I'd have if I just let myself work on Sundays. But I've stuck to it, even after my parents stopped making me, and even when everyone around me thinks I'm crazy.

I see exhaustion everywhere, in myself and in my friends. We stay up all night working or bingeing Netflix, searching for ways to either get work done faster or to avoid it. We waste hours and hours, then have to pay for our procrastination when the deadlines loom. And even our time spent not working drains us. Reading the endless stream of bad news that flows in through the internet is exhausting. Cataloguing likes on Instagram is exhausting. Even as we're trying to relax, stress creeps in.

If we make our devices the center of our universe, we'll end up lonely and burned out.

So please, even if you ignore everything else in this book, consider taking a Sabbath. Sabbaths are a gift, a true and joyous gift from God. We get to simply rest. And if we want to rest, we should be careful about tech.

It's so tempting to go straight to my phone when I'm tired, when I need to turn off my brain. When I've had a rough day,

How Often Does Your Family
Do Any of the Following Together?
(showing percent who do this at least weekly)

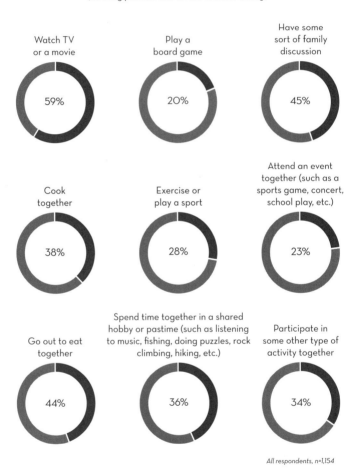

Watch TV or a movie — 59%

Play a board game — 20%

Have some sort of family discussion — 45%

Cook together — 38%

Exercise or play a sport — 28%

Attend an event together (such as a sports game, concert, school play, etc.) — 23%

Go out to eat together — 44%

Spend time together in a shared hobby or pastime (such as listening to music, fishing, doing puzzles, rock climbing, hiking, etc.) — 36%

Participate in some other type of activity together — 34%

All respondents, n=1,154

the last thing I want is to do anything more difficult than flopping on my couch and staring at a screen. But I want to feel more than just momentarily distracted. I want that ten-hours-of-sleep feeling, that just-got-back-from-the-mountains feeling, when I feel brand-new inside and out.

It's difficult to rest sometimes; rest requires sacrificing what we enjoy and what we hate and what we have to do. But the sacrifices we make pale in comparison to the boundless gifts of rest.

What kinds of gifts? For me, there's one Sabbath ritual that's an icon of the grace of Sabbath.

It began around the time I turned eleven years old. I had just discovered my skill in making fancy desserts—I had always loved food, but I had only recently started to gain the skills necessary to craft delicacies like pistachio chocolate éclairs and three-layer strawberry cakes.

It seemed appropriate to have a fancy meal to go with a fancy dessert. Add to that my family's love of caffeine, and you get the pinnacle of our Sunday afternoons, the highlight of the week, and the most ridiculous and wonderful family ritual imaginable: Sunday afternoon tea.

The planning for Sunday tea would begin early in the week with the crafting of the menu. Mom would help me narrow down a wide selection of extravagant dessert recipes, and we'd settle on some reasonably nutritious foods to accompany the sweets. On Saturday, Mom would go grocery shopping, often taking me along to persuade her to buy extra treats;

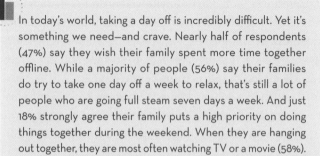

In today's world, taking a day off is incredibly difficult. Yet it's something we need—and crave. Nearly half of respondents (47%) say they wish their family spent more time together offline. While a majority of people (56%) say their families do try to take one day off a week to relax, that's still a lot of people who are going full steam seven days a week. And just 18% strongly agree their family puts a high priority on doing things together during the weekend. When they are hanging out together, they are most often watching TV or a movie (58%).

when we got home, we'd type up our menu on her laptop in a fancy font.

On Sunday, we'd return from church with a purpose. For an hour or two, Mom would garden, Dad would nap, Timothy would play music, and I would fight the anticipation. Then began the preparation of the feast! There were almost always scones, our favorite triangular oatmeal scones with a sprinkle of brown sugar streusel. There were the fancy desserts: éclairs, apple turnovers, lemon mousse, or some other delightful extravagance. Then, thanks to Mom, there were always fruits and vegetables—but dressed up, the veggies cut into artful slices and drizzled with hummus or olive oil, the fruits juicy and fresh and swirled into flowers. And then some small bowls of soup or little triangle sandwiches for when we actually got hungry.

Five minutes before teatime, Dad would brew up a pot or two of tea. He'd make a pot of Earl Grey for himself and Mom, and lemon tea, ginger tea, or rooibos tea for my brother and me. We'd sit down, pour our tea, and begin to feast.

Sunday afternoon tea will always mean Sabbath to me. The practices and disciplines that go into the day are all just preparations for a grand feast, a generous feast where nothing is necessary and everything is delightful. In Psalm 127, an ancient poet counsels us: "It is in vain that you rise up early and go late to rest, eating the bread of anxious toil; for [God] gives to his beloved sleep."[6] Sabbath offers us the sleep of the beloved. Sabbath offers us not the bread of anxious toil but the glorious feast of rest.

. . . .

WHAT TO DO NEXT
Practices for Your Tech-Wise Life

» Don't let your phone mess with your sleep. What practices could help? My friend Caroline sets aside the thirty minutes before bed as screen-free time, and I put my phone outside my room (typically downstairs) before I get ready for bed. To wake up, try using an alarm clock! I have one that lets me set three alarms, enough for even the sleepiest of mornings.

» Pick a day to give up work every week—Saturday or Sunday will probably be best—and recruit your family and friends into joining you. It's going to be a lot harder to rest by yourself. I think having a full twenty-four-hour day is

the richest and most rewarding way, and that might mean
5:00 pm Saturday to 5:00 pm Sunday, if that schedule
works for you.

» Make a plan for how you'll be able to finish your work. My
mom and dad always asked me on Friday, "How are you
going to get your work done before Sunday?" Ask yourself
and others this question.

» Communicate to your family and friends that you're planning not to work one day a week. My friends are happy to
accommodate my Sabbath, and will plan to hang out on
Sunday because they know I'm working on Saturdays, for
example.

» On the night before your Sabbath, put your phone away
(out of your bedroom!) and power off your laptop. They
might be handy during the day, but they should be used
intentionally, not accidentally. It should take a little effort
to access them.

» Put away any signs of homework, if you can. I would always get a little stressed at seeing any unfinished work on
the table.

» Figure out what makes you feel rested—what makes you
feel like *you*. Timothy loves to wash his car on Sundays,
for instance. And my dad always takes a nap.

» Finally, don't let legalism dictate your Sabbath. It's not a
way for you to get more brownie points with God or a sol-
emn self-improvement ritual. It's a gift, like sleep, that will
refresh you. Rest wholeheartedly.

Dear Amy,

You're right—sleep is one of my very favorite things. One of the first verses of the Bible I memorized was that terrific promise from Psalm 127:2: "God gives sleep to those he loves." There are all kinds of things I love to do while I'm awake. But I love the idea even more that every night I get to set all those aside, all my achievements and all my anxieties, and just rest.

But as much as I love sleep, I love Sabbath even more—the day of rest, which our family generally observes on Sundays. As you know, I do enjoy an extra-long nap on many Sundays, but since I sleep (and nap) so much the rest of the week, it's not like I need to catch up on sleep. Sabbath is even better than sleep—it's a day when we can be wide awake and yet resting.

I think a lot of readers (or skimmers) of *The Tech-Wise Family* assume that the thing I'm most suspicious of in the world of technology, or that I'm the most against, is screens—the "glowing rectangles" that we tried to be careful about as you were growing up. But that's not even close to right. The thing I actually abhor more than anything else technology has given us is our restlessness—our Sabbathlessness.

Our lack of Sabbath is deeply connected to the invention of machines and the devices that followed them. Machines don't need to rest. In fact, shutting down a factory one day a week (or even overnight) is incredibly expensive and often hard on the mechanical equipment. So as the world became more and more built for machines, factories started working seven days a week and twenty-four hours a day. That's good for machines (and making money) but terrible for people.

In my lifetime, almost every hint of a day of rest has disappeared from our culture. (The United States seems to be a uniquely restless country. It's not as bad in other countries, even those that have highly developed technology. Much of Europe, for example, is still closed on Sundays, especially outside the tourist centers. Israel largely ceases work every Saturday, and even El Al, the national airline, doesn't fly.) This is bad news in every way. As our friend Matthew Sleeth has noted, if Americans simply observed the Sabbath—resting one day in seven, doing no work and minimizing our consumption and entertainment—it would not only be good for our souls, bodies, and families but dramatically reduce the environmental cost of our way of life. Our lack of a day of rest is especially hard on people who can't set their own work schedules—people who work in stores and restaurants that are open seven days a week. In Deuteronomy, God commands his people to rest, along with every single person and animal in their community, because they were once slaves in Egypt—never having a day of rest is a lot like being enslaved, and God never wanted anyone, even the servants of the Israelites, to experience that again. But in our country, almost everyone keeps up a frantic pace of work and consumption seven days a week.

I think I understand why. If you don't have something to fill the day with, a day of rest can sound boring (there's that modern idea again). But just as God didn't have to "rest" from creation because he was tired, so the main reason for us to have a Sabbath from all our work (including the work our devices do for us and the ways they entertain us) is not to recover from exhaustion—that's what nightly sleep is for—but to be able to properly celebrate life in God's world.

If I could change only one thing in our tech-foolish world, it wouldn't be to take away all the screens: it would be to take away all the restless activity one day a week (which would indeed involve turning off the screens, but just for a day). I actually think that if we did that, the rest of the week would completely change for everyone. I know it would, because this is one thing our family has learned to do, and it's made the rest of our life together so much better. I just hope that over

time many more people will join us in reclaiming the
great gift of resting, feasting, and celebrating, without
anyone or anything having to work on our behalf.

Love,
Dad

8

we can live in hope

Dear Amy,

Let's do this final chapter differently. I want to give you the very last word—partly because I've skipped ahead, and the last word you have to say is so good. And really, what is worse than a parent (or anyone else) who always thinks they have to have the last word? So I'm writing this letter at the beginning of this chapter instead of the end.

Maybe this is the place to confess that I worry a bit about this book. With *The Tech-Wise Family*, I had two big fears. I was afraid that parents would feel guilty reading it—like they hadn't done what they could have to make their homes the best possible places for their kids to grow up. Parents, believe it or not, feel that kind of guilt all the time, for so many different reasons. And while guilt often alerts us that something is truly wrong, on its own it rarely leads us to change. I didn't want to leave anyone with that feeling.

I also worried about what kids would think of the book—I think I imagined they'd forever after remember my name as the author of "that red book that ruined my life after my mom and dad read it." (That has happened, I'm afraid! But I've also met a lot of kids, like you, who are so glad their family is on a tech-wise path.)

With this book, my fear is different. You've done such a great job of writing about the risks of technology without condemning it, I almost worry you've been too easy on it (and on us).

I have no interest in condemning technology either—I'm writing these very words on a glowing rectangle, after all, and you've seen up close that I am one of the world's great tech geeks. Our family never set out to eliminate any kind of technology—though we have great respect for our neighbors, like the Amish, who do. We just sought, and still seek, to keep it in its proper place.

But I worry that a lot of kids and adults will finish this book, breathe a sigh of relief that they don't have to throw all their devices away—and not realize how hard it is to live the life you've described.

I worry that we underestimate how much technology is stealing from us—all of us, since hardly anything in this book applies only to kids—and how challenging it is to get real life back.

I worry most of all, to be honest, that a lot of kids don't know what they are missing—that they haven't even once been on a mountain at sunrise, made a cake from scratch, played music on an instrument they practiced for years, or had a dinner by candlelight with their family. More deeply, I am afraid that our world, with its constantly glowing lights, never lets us see either how dark the world can get or how glorious it can be. That we live with so much noise we don't know what silence sounds like, let alone that taking the time to be truly silent allows us to discover we are not alone but that Another is with us, is speaking to us, and loves us.

I worry readers will finish this and say that dismissive phrase we hear so often these days: "I'm good."

I don't think we're good.

I think before I was even born, our culture took some seriously wrong turns with technology. We could have had a lot of its benefits and still kept the silence, still kept the dark night sky, still made our own music, still hiked up to the peak in the pre-dawn twilight. But instead we let most of those things slip away. Your generation, in particular, is paying the price for all of that, and you are feeling it deep in your souls in ways no one else has up to now.

Of all the things I'm glad and grateful for, one is that you, somehow, escaped. You had some really tough moments as you grew up—some tough years. But you have come out on the other side, on the threshold of twenty years old, more joyful and bold and confident than I ever dared to hope.

I want every kid who reads this book to know that kind of life.

I hope that a lot more people will join us in being tech-wise. I actually dare to hope that a lot of kids who read this will be the ones to help their whole family, including their parents, move toward the life that really is life. It's so easy to give up on one another, even in our families, and think we'll never be more than we are. I think there's a lot of families, of all kinds, that could experience so much more of life together.

And now that I've confessed my fear that we'll settle for less, let me say, too, that as we finish this book together, I have hope that is much stronger than fear. The story of technology is not over—it's just barely started. I think a lot of us are going to make very different choices than we did in the past. I think we all still have time to turn this story around.

And I'm glad we get to do it together.

Love,
Dad

[Amy again]

A few weeks ago, I had to get a tooth filled. I went to the dentist's office, lay back in the chair, and prepared for my fate.

The first thing the dentist did, as usual, was inject my jaw with anesthetic. Pretty soon I was numbed up—all I had to do was stay still while drills whirred around in my mouth. I didn't feel anything.

Once my dentist had set and polished up the filling, I was ready to go. I asked my dentist how soon I could eat—my stomach was grumbling. "Well," he said, "technically, now is fine. The filling is hardened, so nothing bad will happen to it if you eat. But if you don't wait until the numbness is gone, you might bite yourself while you chew without noticing—and then you'd come yell at me for something I didn't do."

Because I was numb, I was at risk of hurting myself. I was at risk of not knowing what my body felt; I couldn't fully tell where my tongue and cheek and molars were, let alone whether they were injured. The anesthetic kept me from pain but also made me less aware of myself—with potentially painful results.

The power to numb is one of technology's most tempting promises. Our devices are pretty great at making our lives easier. They entertain us; they distract us. They help smooth away the annoyances and inconveniences of life.

But if we don't pay attention to what our devices are doing, we can hurt ourselves. I wouldn't have wanted to get a filling without being numbed—that would have been a nightmare. But that anesthetic wasn't random; my dentist chose the medication carefully and injected it only to the area that needed it. If my dentist had given me too much or too little, or hadn't told me how to take care of myself in the meantime, I could have been badly hurt.

I hope we can learn to treat technology with this kind of care and responsibility. I know for a fact it won't come naturally. When I'm upset, my fingers itch to click on a YouTube video or a playlist or scroll through social media. At the end of a long day, flopping on the couch to binge on TV sounds pretty great.

Tech can make life so easy. But if we try to make life too easy—to numb away all the pain and difficulties of our lives—it might backfire. In the long run, it's worth paying attention to the wounds we accumulate in our day-to-day lives, so that we can fix them.

This takes real courage; I'd be lying if I didn't say that a tech-wise life is, in some ways, harder than a high-tech one. Courage means embracing the failures ahead before knowing what they are. That's hard. Numbing our fears is easy and quick; an honest struggle with our pain doesn't seem to fit into our busy days.

Being tech-wise also forces us to relinquish control. Tech sure makes it seem like we're in charge, but the truth is we'll never have as much control over our futures as we'd like. As a Christian, I have faith there is One who does have ultimate authority. God can give me what I need. I can't. Tech can make our lives seem easier and safer, but it can't put us in charge.

I am so, so grateful for the ways in which technology has made my life less painful and difficult. Many people—many kids my age—haven't had this help. If my gratitude ever fails for the baffling gifts I've been given, I don't deserve them.

Yet for all the goodness of these gifts, they cannot be anything more than accessories to the choices I make. Tech can help me build a life worth living, but it can never be the foundation—no amount of tech can replace the hard and lovely work of building a community and following God. I have tried to refrain from blanket statements about tech in this book, but I want this to be crystal clear: we cannot build our lives on the promises of tech. If we put weight on them, those promises will collapse.

In trying (and failing, and trying again) to live a tech-wise life, I am trying to live so that I don't look to my devices for ultimate help. I am trying to cultivate the trust it takes to live a truly good life, trust in the God who will support me when no tech can. I choose to refuse tech's offers of security so that I can face the world with courage.

• • •

When this book is published, I'll be twenty years old. I'll have officially left my teen years behind; now, as a nineteen-year-old, I'm feeling the end is near.

The past years of being a teenager? They've been a lot. They've been wrenching. They've been thrilling. They've shaken me to my core, and I've had to put myself back together. Growing up is a wild ride, with pain and joy around every corner.

Unlike any other generation in history, you and I are growing up with this crazy, powerful new force of technology. And our parents don't always understand it. We should surely listen to wisdom from older family and friends, but we're the ones who have the power—and the responsibility—to choose how to live with it.

As I've tried to make clear throughout this book, it's not just about the phones in our pockets or the iPads on our couches. Barring catastrophes outside our control, we can safely assume that our future will be full of technology. But we *can* control the way we choose to shape our world. Will we let tech determine how we live our lives, or will we be in charge?

Make no mistake: tech isn't neutral. It makes a whole lot of assumptions about who we are and how we want to live our lives. What would it look like if we let our devices control us? Let's think about what the coders in Silicon Valley have decided we need. What does tech say about who we are?

It says we're *busy*. It says we don't have the time to think deeply, nor do we have the time for conversations. We need to multitask to survive. We need task-managing apps, we need news summaries, we need CliffsNotes. Tech says there aren't enough hours in the day. We need our email open until midnight, our work on Google Drive being frantically edited into the wee hours.

And it says that we're *bored.* Isn't that interesting? In techno-world, we're both bored and busy. We're working long hours, but we need a break; we need labor-saving devices because we hate our labor. In response, technology provides more entertainment than all the humans on Planet Earth could ever watch. It presumes we need distraction and diversion, as much as possible. It gives us games to play on the bus and TV to binge at night. Tech says we're bored and need something to fill that space—fast.

And our technology assumes we're *lonely.* We need companionship, so tech provides virtual intimacy. We need people who agree with us, so tech insulates echo chambers for us. We're far away from the people we care about, so tech gives us social media and texts and phone calls, because we can't see them in person when we need them.

You can probably think of other assumptions too. Tech assumes that we're anxious, that we're envious, that we're unsafe, that we're exhausted. It assumes, in other words, that we need saving.

Is this wrong?

The designers of our apps and devices have figured something out. Look around at our generation. We *are* busy. We *are* bored. And we *are* very, very lonely. We're constantly being rushed around to school and work and sports and clubs, yet many of us are also doubtful any of the drudgery of school will pay off. And our generation is deeply, devastatingly lonely. Looking at it this way, life can seem pretty bad.

We have to confront these real problems; tech might be an accessory to them, but it's not really the cause. Yet we also need to confront tech. Just like the anesthesia for my tooth filling, it can help camouflage our problems. It can persuade us that these issues are the new normal—that we just have to live with them. Boredom, busyness, and loneliness, they're just how life is, says tech; all we can do is put a Band-Aid on them and ignore the pain.

• • •

I am determined not to give in. Let's fight boredom every time it rears its head. I walk past the same trees every day on my way to school; I see the same people every week. Yet every day I marvel to learn something new about a friend I've known for ages. And on a sunny morning, every glittering blade of grass looks brand-new.

Let's fight our busyness too. This isn't something we can do alone, and it's not something tech can do for us. I believe part of the answer is found in community. With my family and friends, I can talk honestly about the pursuits filling up my days and squeezing out my hours of rest. I need to be told the truth that a life full of stress isn't sustainable. And I need my community to support me, to take some of my responsibilities when I'm overwhelmed, to help me rest.

Loneliness is, I think, the hardest of all. Loneliness followed me closely when I was a teen, as it did most people I know. And it can destroy us like nothing else can. Slowly, though, I've emerged from it. I have plunged deeply into community and discovered what a lie it is that I am ever alone. I have set aside the endless visions of friends on my screens and sought the real thing. I have learned to take a deep breath and take the great risk of getting to know someone.

You, too, have felt the deep pain that tech tries to hide. I don't know how. But I know that tech will not be able to save you from the anxiety that keeps you up at night or the hurt that breaks your heart.

Here is what I want you to know: we can shake off our fears like the dust on our feet.

I can honestly say that my life has more confidence and wonder and rest than it did four years ago. I wake up with hope in my heart. I am no longer lonely. I rejoice in myself and in those around me.

Our generation is indeed facing great struggles, and not only from tech. Sometimes it seems impossible that the darkness over us will lift. Sometimes fear seems to be our only future. Sometimes it seems impossible that we could ever be anything but busy, lonely, and bored.

But I don't have to be.

You don't have to be.

We don't have to be.

Amy's acknowledgments

Many thanks to the team at Barna Group who first thought it might be a good idea for me to write a book, especially David Kinnaman and Bill Denzel. (And thanks to Emily Kinnaman for showing me the beautiful California coast after long brainstorming sessions!) Thanks to Roxanne Stone for her creative, tough, and kind edits and her addition of data—without Roxy there would be fewer stories and far more abstract rambling. To Kathy Helmers, for being a great agent and helping a totally inexperienced author figure out the crazy world of publishing!

Thanks also to the team at Baker Publishing Group, especially Rebekah Guzman, for taking on this project from an eighteen-year-old. Many thanks to Jamie Chavez for the several rounds of edits, taking on puzzling phrasing and inconsistencies with aplomb. To the design, marketing, and production teams, thank you for turning this manuscript from a Word document into a real, gorgeous book.

And so many thanks to all my dear friends and mentors in Ithaca who brought me tea, sat by me while I wrestled with sentences, and gave me hugs: especially Laurie for her never-ending encouragement, Nicole for her gift of listening, and Hannah for our Wednesday mornings full of mundane and profound talks. Special thanks to the people who shared their stories for the book: Bethany, Carley, Jeremy, Caroline, and Abby.

And of course, my family: Mom, Dad, and Timothy, thank you for your patience and your love.

notes

A letter to Amy

1. 1 Timothy 6:19 NRSV.

Chapter 2 we don't have to be distracted

1. *Dictionary of the Middle Ages*, s.v. "Chained Books," ed. Joseph R. Strayer (New York: Scribner, 1982).

2. Laura L. Bowman et al., "Can Students Really Multitask? An Experimental Study of Instant Messaging While Reading," *Computers & Education* 54, no. 4 (May 2010): 927–31; Joshua S. Rubinstein et al., "Executive Control of Cognitive Processes in Task Switching," *Journal of Experimental Psychology: Human Perception and Performance* 27, no. 4 (2001): 763–97.

3. J. Whitmel Earley, *The Common Rule: Habits of Purpose for an Age of Distraction* (Downers Grove, IL: InterVarsity, 2019), 63.

Chapter 3 we don't have to be disconnected

1. Sherry Turkle, *Reclaiming Conversation: The Power of Talk in a Digital Age* (New York: Penguin, 2015), 153.

2. J. Matthew Sleeth, *Serve God, Save the Planet: A Christian Call to Action* (Hartford, VT: Chelsea Green, 2006), 97.

3. K. Schwab, "Nest Founder: 'I Wake Up in Cold Sweats Thinking, What Did We Bring to the World?," *Fast Company*, July 7, 2017, https://www.fastcompany.com/90132364/nest-founder-i-wake-up-in-cold-sweats-thinking-what-did-we-bring-to-the-world.

Chapter 4 we don't have to live with secrets

1. Maggie Jones, "What Teenagers Are Learning from Online Porn," *New York Times*, February 7, 2018, https://www.nytimes.com/2018/02/07/magazine/teenagers-learning-online-porn-literacy-sex-education.html.

2. Caitlin Dewey, "The Only Guide to Gamergate You Will Ever Need to Read," *Washington Post*, October 14, 2014, https://www.washingtonpost.com/news/the-intersect/wp/2014/10/14/the-only-guide-to-gamergate-you-will-ever-need-to-read/.

3. Genesis 16:13 NIV.

Chapter 5 we don't have to edit our lives

1. Exodus 20:17.

2. C. S. Lewis, *The Voyage of the Dawn Treader* (New York: HarperTrophy, 1994 [1952]), 183.

Chapter 6 we don't have to avoid boredom

1. Apparently one of the girls takes the basket with her. Seems a bit rude, but okay.

2. Gerard Manley Hopkins, "God's Grandeur," accessed May 4, 2020, https://www.poetryfoundation.org/poems/44395/gods-grandeur.

Chapter 7 we don't have to be exhausted

1. T. Rodriguez, "Without Enough Sleep, Teenagers' Mental Health Suffers," *Scientific American Mind* 26, no. 4 (2015): 18.

2. "Why Do We Need Sleep?" National Sleep Foundation, accessed December 23, 2019, https://www.sleepfoundation.org/articles/why-do-we-need-sleep.

3. S. Royant-Parola, V. Londe, S. Tréhout, and S. Hartley, "The Use of Social Media Modifies Teenagers' Sleep-Related Behavior," *Encephale* 44, no. 4 (2018): 321–28.

4. Exodus 20:8–11.

5. Donna Freitas, *The Happiness Effect: How Social Media Is Driving a Generation to Appear Perfect at Any Cost* (New York: Oxford University Press, 2017).

6. Psalm 127:2.

AMY CROUCH is a student at Cornell University studying linguistics, English, and anything else she can fit into her schedule. She loves to cook, climb mountains, and chat about books.

ANDY CROUCH is an author, speaker, musician, and dad. In addition to his books, *The Tech-Wise Family*, *Culture Making*, *Playing God*, and *Strong and Weak*, his work has been featured in *Time*, the *Wall Street Journal*, the *New York Times*, and Lecrae's 2014 single "Non-Fiction." He is partner for theology and culture with Praxis.

BARNA GROUP is a social research company that tries to see the big picture of trends that impact our daily lives. In order to understand what young people are feeling and experiencing, we talked to a lot of teens and young adults, ages thirteen to twenty-one (1,154 of them, to be exact). The group we interviewed comes from across the United States and was randomly selected to represent the whole population of thirteen- to twenty-one-year-old Americans. Taking this kind of scientific approach to social research lets readers like you compare your experiences to the larger national average.

Barna works with lots of different people and organizations to do social research. If you like this kind of geeky stuff, check out what we're doing at www.barna.com.

We also work with young people and parents to help them to identify their deepest motivations and understand how that might influence what they do with their lives. You can learn more at www.trumotivate.com.

Tech-wise principles for
THE WHOLE FAMILY!

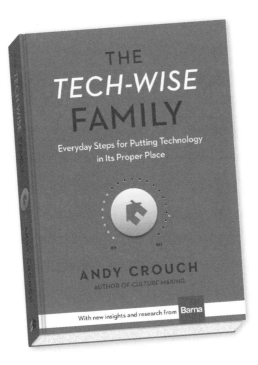

Drawing on in-depth original research from the Barna Group,
Andy Crouch shows readers that the choices we make about
technology have consequences we may never have considered.
Anyone who has felt their family relationships suffer or their time
slip away amid technology's distractions will find in this book a
path forward to reclaiming their real life in a world of devices.

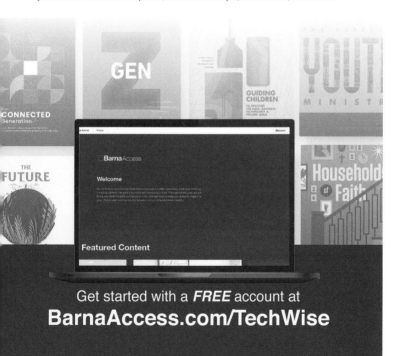